EXPOSING THE BIGGEST PROBLEM
IN DENTISTRY AND HOW TO SOLVE IT

DENTAL
DISORDER

Dr Cohen-
Thank You For
Improving Dentistry!
—Bryan

DR. BRYAN LASKIN

EXPOSING THE BIGGEST PROBLEM IN DENTISTRY AND HOW TO SOLVE IT

DENTAL DISORDER

DR. BRYAN LASKIN

DENTAL DISORDER

EXPOSING THE BIGGEST PROBLEM IN DENTISTRY
AND HOW TO SOLVE IT

DR. BRYAN LASKIN

230 Manitoba Ave South, Suite 110
Wayzata, MN 55391
upgradedental.com

ISBN hardcover 978-1-7366437-3-0
ISBN paperback 978-1-7366437-4-7
ISBN eBook 978-1-7366437-5-4

This book is dedicated to my hero and grandfather, George Bernstein. He fueled my love of reading and is the model by which I try to conduct myself in business and life.

Just by buying this book, you've already made a difference. 100% of the proceeds of Dental Disorder are going to support the not-for-profit Dental Standards Institute and its work to remove the bottlenecks to innovation within healthcare and to put patients first.

To get involved, join us at:

DentalStandardsInstitute.com

DISCLAIMER

This publication contains the opinions and ideas of its author. It is intended to provide helpful content for the purpose of elevating patient care and increasing joy and fulfillment throughout the healthcare profession with an emphasis on the dental industry.

There are strong opinions in this book which are true at the time of its publication. It is the author's sincere hope that we, the dental industry, act swiftly to make much of this content outdated which would, obviously, result in a changing of the convictions held within.

Within this book, the author may discuss companies and entities in which he holds financial interest and such interests are disclosed when the entities are first mentioned. All the names are fictional, unless permission for their use has been granted. Nonspecific pronouns have been utilized in an attempt to convey a more realistic nature to any analogies. In cases where characteristics of fictional characters are portrayed, there has not been any intent to omit or otherwise exclude or over use identifications of any type. The

CONTENTS

PREFACE

"First they ignore you, then they laugh at you, then they fight you, then you win."

- Mahatma Gandhi

First off, I would like to extend my gratitude and appreciation to you, the reader, for picking up this book. Just picking up a book about the dental industry, cracking open the spine and reading this far (the first paragraph) shows you are more engaged than the majority of people who are touched by dentistry. And everyone is touched by dentistry in some way.

Therefore, reader, you are likely an exceptional person.

We are about to embark on a journey together that will unveil what I believe to be the single most broken aspect of the dental industry. If you are a dentist, that means that this book addresses what is potentially the single most destructive force that is working against your dental practice, endangering both your practice and the health of your patients.

If you are a vendor to the dental industry—whether an insurance provider, distributor, manufacturer or materials developer—this unnecessary barrier to improving dental practice wellness also impacts your business in a significant and negative way.

Most importantly, I firmly believe that this is the largest barrier to improving the oral wellness of every patient, regardless of whether they regularly see a dentist or not.

There is a moronic state-of-being that we, as an industry, propagate through our continued ignorance or tolerance of it. Those knowingly continuing this problematic reality do so for the most basic of reasons: greed.

In this book, I will unveil the magnitude of this problem and how every patient and every practice is dramatically worse off due to the persistence of archaic solutions we permit to be sold to us for way too much money. This ultimately has fabricated a virtual prison of our work that we pay handsomely for, while some of the most trusted companies in dentistry lock away the key to quality patient care and profitability in a jail that exists within the walls of our practices.

I will expose the tactics that companies use to treat the caring members of our community as work geldings while they profit from our labor and our patients' property, and why we continually pay these companies obscenely high fees.

I call this problem the Dental Disorder. It is a problem that is easy to understand once you learn to see through the cascading mess of sleight-of-hand "dental tricks" that a select few corporations supplying our profession have employed either knowingly, or, in some cases, due to plain old ignorance.

I will be exposing dental vendor business strategies and policies that hurt patients, drain practice revenue and choke innovation.

Fortunately, there are simple solutions to our Dental Disorder. These easy answers will lead to considerable breakthroughs for your practice, saving everyone money, increasing patient access to care and facilitating what we all know needs to happen on behalf of our patients: innovation and medical-dental integration.

Many of the solutions we discuss in this book will be able to be applied immediately to improve the quality of the care you provide, decrease your stress, remove inefficiencies within your team and make more money while spending less.

Outside the walls of the dental practice, our digital life has seen tremendous growth. The first iPhone came out in the year 2007, and the Apple App Store was released the next year in 2008.

Just think about all the updates, transformative applications and major yearly improvements that have transpired since the initial launch of smartphones. These changes spawn lines that wrap around the block, filled with people eager to secure the newest iPhone release. That is some serious innovation and competition for some great software to be developed. While you could argue whether the smartphone has been a net positive for society, its progression into an indispensable tool is undebatable.

But if you look at the technology that runs your practice, it likely does not look or work much different from how it looked and worked at the turn of the century. This is a direct result of the Dental Disorder.

Dental practices and dental patients deserve better.

That is why I have made it my personal mission to fix this Dental Disorder as quickly and effectively as possible.

Before we dive into the Disorder and discuss the solution to the practice-eroding, patient-frustrating practices associated with it, I would like to tell you a story.

It's the story of how I came to care so much about fixing this problem in the first place. It's the story of what made me rethink what I know about how major institutions in our industry act and work with us.

If you told me five years ago that I would be working on Standards development at the highest level in our profession, trading emails with leaders in the Health and Human Services (HHS), collaborating with military information leaders or attending healthcare data conferences acting to connect medicine and dentistry, I would have laughed.

So how did I get involved in this groundbreaking, yet extremely nerdy and highly technical aspect of dentistry?

How did I discover that there were gigantic knowledge gaps at the highest levels of our profession and nefarious operators within our most trusted industry partners who knowingly erode our profession with their selfish business practices?

How did I end up here, writing to you right now with the goal of exposing and correcting the largest disorder within our profession?

How did I reach the point of feeling compelled to educate the dental profession about aspects that are destroying our ability to innovate, even at the risk of corporate retaliation by some of the largest partners I work with in dentistry?

As Theodore Roosevelt said, "In any moment of decision, the best thing you can do is the right thing. The worst thing you can do is nothing".

Therefore, I believe that staying silent, doing nothing, would be the worst thing I could do.

Like everyone, the position I am in is the result of all the decisions I have made up to this point in time. I rely heavily on my intuition when making decisions. Obviously, I put much thought into my decision making, but I also believe that we get so much data input that our brains cannot intelligently process it all.

At that point, if you keep your mind open to creative thinking and have focused goals in mind, your subconscious can successfully guide the processing of information. This is that "gut feeling" that seems to intuitively make sense, especially in particularly challenging situations.

This can create the circumstances for you to seize a moment that feels like a fundamental opportunity to do things a better way. A singular moment that you can capture to improve your life, as well as the lives of others.

We all have experiences like this. An experience in which a painful event leads to growth. As Marcus Aurelius stated, "what stands in the way becomes the way."

In other words, overcoming your problems is the most direct way to capitalize on opportunities, as long as you are armed with the right mindset.

You see, I have been unwittingly preparing to write this book through privileged yet extremely painful interactions with some of the most influential people in dentistry.

Experiences like growing an extremely successful small group of practices, serving as a contrarian within the leadership team at one of the largest DSOs, being an advisor for large dental laboratories and manufacturers, and serving as a board member of several companies while also developing a few of the most innovative solutions in dentistry over the last decade have opened doors for me to hidden rooms in our industry that few get to enter.

In these gatherings, the conversations rarely are about quality of care or how to improve dental practices.

It is all about business. And business (for them) is good.

Some of the most bizarre, frustrating and disappointing conversations I have had with leaders in our industry have fueled the fire within me to expose the opportunities that we all have to lead a better life through dentistry by uncovering these leaders' dirty little secrets.

In the past, I couldn't decide which was worse: the industry leader that is mindfully screwing everyone over or the lazy, ignorant leader that isn't even aware of the problems happening under their nose.

Hint: it's the first one.

Don't get me wrong; most of the companies I have had the honor to work with are filled with phenomenal people who excel at their job. Most of the people in dentistry truly do care about the people they serve.

However, as the mental scars I bear prove, simply wanting to be an innovative technology company or calling yourself one does not make it so. There is a tremendous amount of work, knowledge, skills and risk tolerance involved in innovation, and frankly, most companies that see themselves as innovative just aren't.

Some things cannot be successfully bought, borrowed or stolen. No matter how big you think your company is.

I like to equate great technology to a novel or symphony. It is the people and the environment that make the magic happen. No matter how expensive your pen is, it will not write the next great tragedy for you. The largest budget does not make the best movies without a script and the best talent to back it up. Spending tons of money and copying The Matrix will probably result in the next movie flop (or let's face it, the second Matrix movie).

Before we will get into the finer details, I would like to give you a sneak peek at the problems and solutions that I will be discussing throughout the next several chapters.

You will learn:

- Why the data contained within (and know-ingly excluded from) your PMS is the biggest drain on the quality and quantity of the care you provide and how you can correct this
- What the difference between a "Practice Management System" (PMS) and an Electronic Dental Record (EDR) is and why the concepts of both are broken
- What Standards are and how they are a sig-nificant aspect of dentistry that can directly improve your practice, patient experiences and profitability everyday
- How you are unknowingly, indirectly pay-ing fees that add extra cost into the "dental software tax" and how to avoid them
- How information blocking is used in den-tistry to immorally inflate corporate profits while directly degrading the quality of care our patients receive
- Why dentists do not, in fact, suck at business
- Why our teenagers can use massive con-sumer and educational applications at home and school with zero IT company interven-tion, yet our offices are beholden to exter-nal "experts" that often charge hundreds, if not thousands, of dollars every month to do very similar tasks
- Why dental "insurance" is an even bigger scam than most people realize

- What true interoperability is and why now is the time to incorporate it into your practice

As we start this journey together, I want to thank you again for your interest in bettering dentistry for yourself, your team and, most importantly, for the patients we have the honor to serve.

1

THE STANDARD DISORDER

"The task of leadership is to create an alignment of strengths so strong that it makes the system's weaknesses irrelevant."

- Peter Drucker

Problem: Dentistry has historically been slow to implement Standards that align our profession in several key aspects of our industry, particularly in the areas of emerging technologies and patient advocacy.

Solution: Understand what Standards are, get involved in the underserved initiatives of dental Standard development and/or patient advocacy and leverage technologies that adhere to Standards that elevate our profession.

Like HIPAA and data privacy, dental Standard development has to be one of the least sexy and most mundane and snooze-inducing topics on planet Earth.

And I love them. Especially Standard development.

How did I get so passionate about a topic that, at first glance, seems so boring? Well, I discovered the simple fact that Standards were a pathway to supercharging my true passion: innovation.

Standards allow for faster technological development by aligning an industry through the provision of specifications that can be used consistently to ensure that any product or service is fit for their purpose. You can think of a Standard as an agreed-upon formula for the best way to do something.[1]

It is like defining the building blocks for what you are producing, so you can get on with creating some transformative technology using those blocks.

While it is common to use both lowercase "s" and uppercase "S" when discussing Standards, I would like to clarify why I personally like using the uppercase "S" in the context of ANSI (American National Standards Institute) or ISO Standards.

---

[1] While not exactly a quote, the previous two sentences are a rephrasing of the definition of a Standard from the website of the organization that administers and coordinates U.S. Standards, The American National Standards Institute (ANSI).

The word "standard" gets thrown around and misused quite often, much like the words "literally," "synergy," "AI," "collaboration," "cosmetic dentistry," "med spa" and "rockstar".

Misuse of any word can obfuscate the true meaning of the term. Take, for example, the word "literally." While this word is supposed to be used to describe things in a non-metaphorical way, people use it to emphasize metaphorical and figurative statements.

Similarly, it is correct to call Lenny Kravitz a Rockstar. Your amazing, talented dental assistant is, on the other hand, a rockstar. The capitalized version is factual, while the lowercase version is descriptive.

"Lenny Kravitz is obviously a musical legend. However, you may not know he is also an innovator in dental care. He is Co-Founder of the award winning oral wellness company TWICE, whose charitable work through the Glo Good and Let Love Rule Foundations bring dental care to those in need."

You may have a phenomenal "standard" way of bringing new patients into your office or a "standard" way you prep a crown, but these procedures have not been elevated to the level of an accredited industry Standard in the sense of being agreed upon processes that the industry can adopt. This can only be accomplished through an overseeing Standard accreditation society. In the U.S., this is either through ANSI domestically or ISO internationally.

These ANSI and ISO Standards are developed by Industry Standard Development Organizations (SDOs). The SDO organizations' policies and procedures are also overseen by ANSI and/or ISO, as well.

In order to not completely bore you with semantics, I will summarize Standards as *the single agreed upon way to do something within an industry.*

Standards are voluntary, meaning you do not need to follow them, yet there should be only one Standard for each specified process or guideline for an industry.

Examples of common Standards we encounter every day in dentistry include DICOM, the international Standard used to transmit, store, retrieve, print, process and display medical imaging information and JPEG, an image compression Standard. There are many other less easily referenced Standards, but they are always there, consistently ensuring smooth workflows and removing the barriers to innovation.

DENTAL DISORDER

Lesser known dental Standards include those that define endodontic sealing materials, ceramics, determination of color stability, biocompatibility, dental tool specifications and designations for dental implants.

Can you imagine if every dental implant company defined their implant size designations using a different system? If every dental tool manufacturer called their instrument something different? If every imaging system used a different file format? If, instead of a couple of universal shade guides, each and every manufacturer used a different shade system?

We would have disorder... just like we do with dental data.

The funny thing is that when I first got involved with dental Standards, I knew none of this.

I was at a conference promoting OperaDDS, the platform I had created and sold prior to developing Toothapps, and this particular platform included one of the first electronic referral systems in dentistry. Even now, electronic referral systems have pathetically low utilization by dental professions, but the few people that did use our referral system loved it.

At the conference, a nice, forward-thinking dentist came up to me and said, "Bryan, I have a referral system I developed, but everyone in my state uses yours.

Would you be willing to connect our platforms so we could share information back and forth?"

There have been a few times in my life that I have felt a spark of creativity that inspired me to think much bigger than I thought possible and struck me with the image or idea of something that was larger than I could rationally conceive of on my own.

This was one of those times.

For some reason I don't quite understand, I impulsively exclaimed, "Screw that! You and I are the only dentists doing this. Let's create a standard for how this information should be shared!"

At the time, I had absolutely no idea what creating a Standard actually meant, how difficult it would be and how profoundly this concept was needed (hence the lowercase spelling in my quote above).

But something told me at that exact moment that the reason why virtually nobody was using these electronic referral platforms (of which there were about five at the time) was that there was no way for us to share information between all of them. Nobody wants to sign up for a referral system that the other person you are communicating with doesn't want to use.

And this dentist's idea to share information between all of us was the solution.

Here's the problem we were looking to address:

If you used one referral platform, the other person had to be using that same platform or they could not access the referral information. This seemed idiotic to me. Why not have us all agree upon what kind of information should be shared and how we share it?

You may be thinking the same question that many dental software vendors think: "why would you want to work with your competition like that, Bryan?"

Well, that's exactly the self-serving type of thinking that is at the core of the Dental Disorder.

Most software companies act like they own all the information in the referral slip. This is NOT the case. The information is primarily owned by the patient, and the dentist has the authority to share this information as and when they deem it necessary to provide care for their patient.

I firmly believe that the biggest (and often the only real) competition any creative company has is complacency.

Stagnation is the enemy of innovation.

In the case of electronic referrals, the true competition is not other electronic referral platforms; it's a pad of paper and a pen. Dentists having to continue using archaic, pathetic means of communication with the care professionals they collaborate with is what we are truly trying to change.

And all of us who are working to accomplish this must team up because changing people's behavior is the real challenge.

If you could sign up for a free or low-cost electronic referral system and be 100% confident that it would work with all the other dental referral systems on the market, how likely is it that you would be willing to start using it?

What if you knew that the bulk of the information on any electronic referral prescription was automatically filled out and was the same for each referral? For example, imagine all of your endo referral forms requesting all the same information and organized in the same format instead of coming in different formats for each specialist you work with.

This is just one simple example of a Standard that will transform the Dental Disorder into a new era of reliable communication between dentists and other healthcare providers.

I believed in this so strongly that I then spent the next two years going to the American Dental Association Standard Committee on Dental Informatics (ADA SCDI) meetings until I got frustrated enough to call ANSI and ask what it would take to create a new SDO. My frustration with the ADA SCDI was due to the glacial speed at which progress was being made.

If you are nodding in agreement that the ADA moves slowly, please read the rest of the story.

To say that I have been surprised by how my relationship with the ADA has developed would be a drastic understatement and, strangely, it involves an HBO show as inspiration.

You see, my wife has a particular laugh that only comes out when we are watching TV shows. It is more of a belly laugh than her traditional giggle, higher in tone and more substantial than her typical chuckle.

This characteristic guffaw lets me know that whatever is happening on screen is "something stupid that Bryan would do." Unfortunately, this laugh is never wrong.

While this is fairly a common occurrence in our household, some TV characters provoke it with shocking regularity, like the characters Jay Prichett and Roy Kent on *Modern Family* and *Ted Lasso*. But no character prompts my wife to generate this laugh more often than Larry David in *Curb Your Enthusiasm*.

In one pretty, pretty memorable show, Larry gets kicked out of the coffee shop "Mocha Joe's" because he complains that the scones are too muffin-like, the coffee is cold and the table they sit at is wobbly. After Larry gets kicked out of the restaurant, he is fuming mad, until he looks over and sees an empty space available for lease next to the shop that recently banned him.

Over the next few episodes, Larry goes through tre-mendous effort and expense creating his "spite store." To add further insult to "Mocha Joe's," Larry names his coffee shop "Latte Larry's."

Tesa, my wife, was laughing that laugh throughout the entire story arc, as I have launched several "spite stores" in my time.

Validating Tesa's laugh, after a couple conversations with ANSI and scores of hours of research, I decided to do something even more difficult, costly and energy draining than open a coffee shop. I decided to lead the creation of a new Standard Development Organization that would "do things the way they should be done" (much like Larry did on *Curb*).

I didn't care that it would cost tens of thousands of dollars, take years of research and entail mind-numbingly detailed work that I would have to force myself and the amazing Megan on my team to accomplish. This included writing an eighty-plus page develop- mental procedure document.

There was something that wasn't being done as fast as I wanted it done and nobody else was doing anything about it. So I decided I was going to do it myself.

As a first step, I called the dentist that came up to me at the conference and said, "We are doing this! We are going to lead the creation of a new Standard Development Organization focused on removing the barriers to innovation and advocate for patients!" Obviously, these are my two primary passions in dentistry.

He was less than enthusiastic, probably because he is wiser than I am and knew the amount of work that lay ahead of us. As I can be a solid sales person when the situation requires it, he begrudgingly agreed to be part of the initiative, as long as he didn't have to do anything.

Over the next two and a half years that I worked on the project, I continued going to the ADA Standard meetings.

After a few phone meetings, the other dentist dropped out. So, I recruited everyone in dentistry that I could (about thirty people), creating a group of people who are passionate about innovating dentistry to improve patients' experiences.

Thus, Dental Standards Institute, or DSI, was born.

DSI received its ANSI accreditation status and non-profit designation one week before the COVID shut-down. It was like a sign to me that we were on the right path. When the world shut down, I had a new purpose to focus on.

Over the course of the next several months, we developed and submitted Standards that would become ANSI accredited Standards. The initial three Standards were:

DENTAL DISORDER

ANSI/DSI MST1.1:2020
Definitions of Terms In Dental Metrics

- ANSI/DSI MST1.1 lists the definition of terms within the dental industry regarding dental metrics, allowing for accurate dental practice support and consistency in communication and alignment in business systems. These definitions increase dental care quality and ease dentists' ability to evaluate how they can best be of service to the general public.

ANSI/DSI GSST1.1:2020 Graphic Symbols - Pictograms
For Information Regarding the Healthcare Patient

- ANSI/DSI GSST1.1 defines graphic symbolization and pictogram representation of crucial information regarding the healthcare patient. The goal of this Standard is to address the need for easily identifiable, universal communication of information within the electronic health record (EHR), including electronic dental records (EDR), for the purpose of reducing miscommunications within healthcare. This Standard also defines the visualization of crucial graphic symbols within the EHR.

ANSI/DSI VRST1.1:2020 Usage of Therapeutic
Virtual Reality for Anxiety Reduction In Healthcare

- ANSI/DSI VRST1.1 addresses the opportunity that Therapeutic Virtual Reality (TVR) presents, as it has been proven to be effective in treating many cases of anxiety in healthcare. This Standard addresses many concerns that can occur if TVR is applied incorrectly, including TVR's potential to lead to patients getting exposed to nausea-inducing content. Another concern that this Standard directly addresses is the fact that seemingly innocuous content, when displayed in Virtual Reality can also be shocking to which also can have a negative effect on the quality of care. Additionally, infection control protocols for TVR are described.

Based on my experiences and the feedback from the DSI Development Committee, as well as our workgroup committee members, I felt that all of these Standards were vital to align dentistry to improve patient care.

However, the ADA was not convinced at the time. In fact, the ADA deliberated the development process we used at DSI, as well as every one of the Standards we had proposed.

I had worked for over three years to get DSI created and someone else, the ADA, was questioning its validity.

To put it mildly, I was not impressed, and I let them know this in no uncertain terms.

While on these many deliberation calls, I lashed out at the ADA staff and members, partially because I was incensed at being required to explain what we were doing at DSI, and partially because I never thought I would work with the ADA again. Suffice to say, I did not hold back when slinging insults and accusations.

To the immense credit of the incredible volunteer dentists who Co-Chair the ADA SCDI, I believe that impactful positive changes have transformed the ADA Standards development process over the last few years.

In fact, I am happy to report that I have been involved in working groups and Standard development with the ADA, alongside my work at DSI. Standards must strive for everyone to work together in order to reach consensus and this, in my opinion, is a great example of collaboration at work to help our profession.

Together we are developing what I believe will be the key Standards required to align the profession, so that crucial patient electronic dental health information will be available to all dentists and healthcare providers in a format anyone can leverage.

It turns out that combining my experiences as a dentist and serial tech entrepreneur with the talented technical minds I have met along the way and with the industry presence of the ADA resulted in an ideal recipe to design and implement the Standards and applications that are required to solve the Dental Disorder.

There are many, many talented people who are working on these projects. Too many to list here, but I must acknowledge the strength of character of the Co-chairs of the ADA SCDI, Drs. Greg Zeller and Mark Jurkovich.

I also must recognize the technical prowess of Toothapps' CTO and Co-Founder, Aleh Matus, who is, I am sure, one of the most talented software engineers walking planet Earth right now. We in dentistry are lucky to have his mind focused on correcting the Dental Disorder.

The first breakthrough Standard that we are writing is called "ODIN," or the Oral Dataset Interoperability Network.

ODIN's purpose is to provide for the permissioning, authentication and necessity validation for structured electronic data elements, supporting key information exchange among and between dental and other health-care settings. ODIN covers data that can be shared bidirectionally between providers, like essential patient demographic, dental and medical encounter data, as well as patient clinical data in a structured, computable format between dental or other healthcare venues.

The software platforms that leverage the ODIN Standard will therefore belong to a network of like-minded developers that believe in security, privacy and open sharing of ePHI between dentists, patients and other healthcare providers.

ODIN is not meant to replace existing interoperability Standards in medicine, like FHIR. Instead, its goal is to enhance interoperability for dental patients and professionals.

ODIN is a "behind the scenes" Standard that connects all vital electronic data in dentistry together, as well as connecting dental and medical information.

When using ODIN-approved applications, you will not need to do anything differently from how you do it today. Everything you do will just work better and you will have more accurate and complete data and enhanced access to a new world of information and possibilities for improving your care and production.

And we will be getting rid of the "dental software tax," saving you money.

At this point, allow me to clearly state what the Dental Disorder is.

The electronic Personal Health Information (ePHI) **data contained in dental software systems legally belongs to patients and you, as a dentist, are the steward of this data. Today, however, this vital information is locked in a data prison, blocking access for dentists and patients.**

This explains why:

- You as a dentist have anxiety about leaving the crappy software that sits on the expensive server in your office.
- You have not been able to try out that new, great software that "doesn't integrate" with your Practice Management Software.
- Getting your patient access to their records is a pain in the ass or even impossible.
- You cannot get accurate information (or really any significant info) from the prior dentist when you see a new patient.

- Dental software is hard to use.
- Dental software looks like it was designed alongside Netscape and MySpace.
- Dental software is so damn expensive.

Predatory companies have knowingly subjected you to this garbage while donning a phenomenal costume of sheep's clothing while they perform dental tricks on your practice.

It's time to expose these dental tricks and unveil the solution. The health of your patients and your practice are at risk.

These examples above are a small sampling of how the Dental Disorder negatively affects everyone.

In the chapters that follow, you will learn in more detail:

- What the Dental Disorder is.
- Why you previously have not heard about the Dental Disorder.
- All the ways that the Dental Disorder makes your life harder, costs you money, saps your precious time and hurts the patients you serve.
- The simple solution that addresses the Dental Disorder and how to implement it.

To learn how to get involved in the vital work of Standard development and get your free Dental Disorder Recovery Kit, go to *DentalDisorder.com*

2

THE TYPICAL DISORDER

"Workflow is understanding your job, understanding your tools and then not thinking about it any more."
                                    - Merlin Mann

Problem: Every day in every dental practice, the quality of care and quality of a dental professional's work life are unnecessarily compromised due to illegal, immoral and unethical business practices of some of our most trusted partners in dentistry.

Solution: Exposing the Dental Disorder to be the useless stranglehold on our industry that it is and leveraging interoperable solutions that directly improve our ability to communicate, collaborate and care for patients through Connected Dentistry®.

The Molar Muffin Mishap

Searing pain shot from Lisa's jaw up through the center of her brain. "Owwwwwwww!" she exclaimed as the throbbing commenced and she dropped her blueberry muffin on the floor.

"What's wrong?" asked her husband.

"Something in that muffin crunched, Troy, and now my face feels like it is on fire. Can you call the doctor?"

"Call? Alright, boomer... hold on," Troy joked, while he pulled out his phone and opened his app with a couple of clicks. "Let me take a pic for Dr. Olson over at Lonetree Hospital. Remember, he sure helped with Billy's sinus infection a few years ago."

Lisa opened her mouth and Troy couldn't really see anything, so he flipped on the light on his phone and snapped pictures of Lisa's upper and lower teeth, as well as one of her frowning face (mainly for his own amusement). He then added a quick note to the pics stating, "Lisa lost a fight with a blueberry muffin, Doc, now her face hurts. Can you see anything, or should we come in?"

A slight audio tone went "ping" and the familiar green checkmark let Troy know that Lisa's information was in the right hands.

Troy said in the most reassuring voice he could muster, "Lisa, let's get you some ibuprofen while we wait for Dr. Olson to let us know what to do."

The couple went upstairs to get the ibuprofen, but before they could even find the bottle, Troy's phone buzzed with a message from Dr. Olson's office.

> *"Dr. Olson took a look at the images and it seems like this may be a dental issue. We've already sent your message to your dentist, Dr. Caring. You just need to authorize the transfer, and I'm sure she will get Lisa taken care of right away."*

As if on cue, Lisa's phone started playing the theme to Friends, indicating she had a message. This prompted Troy to complain, "Great, now I will be singing THAT all day!"

Lisa looked at the message and said, "Man, I hope Dr. Caring can help. We should've known this was a dental issue." She then opened the app and authorized her record transfer with three clicks.

After finally finding and taking some ibuprofen (it was in Troy's suitcase from their trip to Bermuda last month), Lisa's phone buzzed again with a message asking Lisa to use the phone's biometric scan to access its contents.

It read:

> *"Lisa, it's Dr. Caring. It looks like that tooth on the lower right that we have been watching over the last couple of years has broken. From the picture you sent and looking at your X-ray here, I think you should see the root canal specialist, Dr. Now. I've already sent a request, so just click on the link below and you can schedule your appointment. Looks like she can see you at 10 or 1 today."*

"Troy, let's get moving… I've got an appointment in 20 minutes!" was the last thing Lisa heard herself saying (with a bit more urgency than was probably required to get her husband moving) before hopping in the car and getting the care she needed.

It was only… Oh, wait. I apologize.

This is not a science fiction novel, nor is it a happy dream I had.

This story obviously did not happen. Lisa's story is not even possible today.

But it should be.

So, please allow me to retell this way-too-common scenario utilizing a more relevant format that depicts how this would actually go down in the real world today, given the current workflows we are stuck using:

Today's Tragic Molar Muffin Mishap

Searing pain shot from Lisa's jaw up through the center of her brain. "Owwwwwwww!" she exclaimed as the throbbing commenced and she dropped her blueberry muffin on the floor.

"What's wrong?" asked her husband.

"Something in that muffin crunched, Troy, and now my face feels like it is on fire. Can you call the doctor?"

After a long pause, Troy sheepishly asked, "Who do we see again?" attempting to mask the fact that he was at least five years overdue for a physical.

"DR. OLSON! Here, the number is in my phone, you troglodyte," Lisa growled in pain and frustration.

After searching for "doctor", "physician" and "hospital" in Lisa's contacts, Troy finally found Dr. Olson's number after typing in "DR".

"...Welcome to Unfair Hospital... due to a recent increase in infections we are experiencing an unusually large volume

of calls… your expected wait time is…TWELVE… minutes…" the robotic voice in the recording chirped.

After a 48-minute hold, being transferred twice and hung up on once, Troy was told that Dr. Olson would be able to see Lisa in two days, and that if that was not acceptable, they should go to urgent care.

Given the level of intense pain, Troy took Lisa to the emergency department at their local hospital. What Troy did not realize is that he was making the same mistake as the two million-plus other people with dental emergencies that end up in the ER each year, to the tune of roughly $750 per visit, totalling a staggering $1.6 billion annually.[1]

As the ER was filled with acute cases, it took over four hours to see the physician, who instantly recognized that Lisa had a dental issue. Obviously, dental care is completely outside of his scope of practice, and as this particular physician had no dental contacts, he simply told Lisa to go call her dentist.

Unfortunately, Lisa's debilitating dental anxiety had prevented her from seeing a dentist for the past five years, so she didn't even have the dental office's contact information in her phone.

It was also a Saturday, so Lisa ended up leaving a message at four different dental practices before finally finding a dentist that picked up her weekend call.

DENTAL DISORDER

After setting up the visit, Lisa parked her car in an expensive ramp and made her way to the practice of the dentist, Dr. Weekend. Dr. Weekend proceeded to take a bitewing and PA radiograph and performed the appropriate endodontic testing.

It took 15 minutes to determine that Lisa's molar was necrotic, and the dentist did not feel comfortable doing the endo. So Dr. Weekend circled #31 on a 4x6 piece of paper (the ★ahem★ "professional" referral slip) and scrawled the word "necrotic" on it alongside Lisa's name and phone number. He then printed off a copy of Lisa's X-rays complete with the white streak lines that announced to the world that his printer was running low on ink.

After his call to the endodontist went to voicemail, Dr. Weekend wrote a prescription for antibiotics and a few pills to help Lisa manage the pain for the next few days.

Dr. Weekend handed Lisa the scribbled referral and prescriptions, cheerfully chirped "good luck with that tooth at Dr. Root's office," and then escorted Lisa out of his practice, reassured in the knowledge that she was now safe in the good hands of Dr. Weekend's friendly neighborhood endodontist (who also happens to have great seats to the Minnesota Wild that she shares with Dr. Weekend a couple of times a year).

Yes, Dr. Weekend's job was done, and a job well done, it was.

Wasn't it?

Let's check back in on Lisa to find out.

At this point, even though Lisa has seen multiple doctors and spent over half a day seeking treatment, she was still in pain. Desperate for relief, Lisa went directly to her favorite pharmacy, filled the prescriptions and left a voicemail for Dr. Root pleading to be seen as soon as possible.

The good news is that Lisa took her meds immediately and started to feel better.

However, when Dr. Root's office called two days later to get her scheduled, she decided she didn't want to waste more time and money seeing doctors who don't solve her problem. Her miserable experience last week more than confirmed that she was right to be so anxious and wary of dentists.

She felt better, thanks entirely to the meds. No thanks to the doctors.

So Lisa confidently crumpled up and threw away her referral slip in the trash. Obviously, she didn't bother to schedule that appointment with the endodontist.

The only other person who knew that Lisa missed her treatment appointment was Lisa's nosey co-worker, Bob, who saw the referral slip and radiographs (which contained her ePHI, obviously) on top of the garbage in the office kitchen.

Lisa then went about her day without realizing that the next time her infection flared, it could close off her airway, in which case an ER visit would be more appropriate (provided she made it there in time).

Of course, neither Dr. Olson, Dr. Weekend nor Dr. Root followed up to prevent such a life-threatening complication from happening, as the software applications they pay several hundred dollars a month for lack the insight required to follow up with Lisa appropriately.

This grim scene obviously doesn't happen with every dental emergency today.

It is estimated, however, that one dental emergency ends up in the emergency department of a hospital every 15 seconds in the U.S.[12] So this scenario is, in fact, quite common.

Let's be optimistic and assume that Lisa was a more compliant/adherent patient and ended up seeing Dr. Root for her root canal.

You may think that our problems end there.

You would be wrong.

---

[2] ADA Health Policy Institute, "Emergency Department Use for Dental Conditions Continues to Increase", Thomas Wall, M.A., M.B.A.; Marko Vujicic, Ph.D., 2015 American Dental Association

Here is a list of just some of the idiotic barriers that we all still endure (I will describe easy solutions to these in the coming chapters):

-   There is no insight into many aspects of the patient's dental insurance and financial arrangements, so errors occur easily between everyone involved (along with massive delays in doctors getting paid).
-   Heaven help us if the patient or one of the healthcare providers would like to have prior authorization of benefits. That EOB? Just an estimate. Case acceptance plummets, the dental insurance plan ultimately pays you whatever they want and it becomes the dentist and/or patient's problem to "fight" for payment.
-   If Lisa cannot verbalize her problem (whether due to anxiety, a medical condition or a lack of the cognitive ability to communicate), all of these problems escalate exponentially, as we have to factor in multiple distinct practices and healthcare providers that can introduce miscommunications and breaks in the patient journey.
-   Lisa may forget about her significant drug allergy (or decide that the "dentist doesn't need to know") when filling out her medical history, thereby putting her at risk for an anaphylactic reaction when taking the prescribed antibiotics (which may not have

even been necessary if she had just seen the endodontist for treatment, in the first place).

- In the best-case scenario we can imagine for Lisa's case today, the risks of taking unnecessary medications and treatments is obscenely unnecessarily high.

- Speaking of unnecessary, today's referral networks require redundant information collection by healthcare providers. This was shown to be a problem in Lisa's case when the endodontist had to take duplicate radiographs to plan this simple case, in order to make up for the poor quality X-ray copies she received which led to poor Lisa getting stuck with increased radiation exposure and added expense.

This simple example of the Dental Disorder alone occurs to an American every 15 seconds all day, every day, all across the country.

The real tragedy here, though, is that the seemingly unattainable first version of our story is entirely possible today. The problem is that we in healthcare, and especially in dentistry, are forced to continue to subject the patients we have the honor of serving to the archaic process depicted in the second version of Lisa's story.

It is time for us to stop tolerating the outdated technology that puts our patients' health at risk, sabotages our profitability and makes us all suffer massive inconveniences due to the poor communication and data transfer capabilities that exist today throughout dentistry, as well as all of healthcare more broadly.

Why are we forced to use this outdated technology? Is it because the better way of doing things is too expensive? Too complicated?

No, the answer is much worse.

Within the dental industry, these chokeholds on innovation have been strangling our practices and quality of care for only one of two reasons:

1) Large industry vendors that have monopolistic levels of market share within the dental industry have knowingly worked to keep these harmful practices in place. They do this because they cannot compete in a landscape where the best products, innovations and technologies are used on behalf of our patients and our practices.

Or

2) Industry vendors remain ignorant to the Dental Disorder outlined in this book. They want to do the best for the practices and patients they serve, but are simply incapable. Don't underestimate the volume of

ignorance and incompetence that balloons within these organizations, especially those that are backed by private equity or that have many mid-level managers and are places where most people show up to work every day just to do the bare minimum and try not to get fired.

These huge companies continue to sell you archaic technology that they often bought after it was already outdated from some innovative company, who knew their solution was becoming outdated even at that time. The innovator walked away with a big check, and the new owner then pushed the technology onto you despite lacking the knowledge or skill required to update it appropriately.

The juggernaut's sole role of owning this acquired technology is to increase their profits and see how much more they can ratchet up the fees.

In full disclosure, I must say here that I have sold several companies and have experience in this game. The big check is always great, however the fallout afterwards has not always been so rosy.

The primary software platform that I sold to one innovative software company actually continued the work that we started and I am proud of what has become of that product and of the service that the customers receive. I look back at the transaction as an incredibly positive experience.

This has not always been the case, however, as evidenced by my transition out of performing clinical dentistry and my experiences taking investments from people and companies that do not understand innovation in dentistry.

Here is what ultimately happens in most cases: a large vendor gobbles up some technology company or solution after the product is past its prime, spreads on a thick layer of monopolistic, anticompetitive business practices on top of this moldy, archaic crap-sandwich and then serves it to you with a label claiming it is the "One Solution for Every Dental Practice."

Oh yeah, and they also charge you around $500 per month to consume this garbage.

They claim there is no need to look outside this old system that has everything you need. They want you to ignore the fact that not one solution in their "shiitake one" platform is best-in-class and that all their "integrations" prove it isn't a unified solution at all.

Their technical prowess is so inadequate that they can't even create a true integration with the platforms they own and control. Remember, they may own it, but they likely didn't create it.

If you bite into this "one easy platform," good luck. You will likely look up and find the only area in which their solutions are actually well designed is in their ability to hold your practice's data hostage.

More accurately, they excel at keeping your patients' and your practice's data out of your hands and out of the hands of your patients.

3

THE DENTIST'S DISORDER

"Straight trees are cut first and honest
people get screwed first."
- Chanakya

Problem: Software in dentistry sucks and is expensive due to the information blocking practice of greedy corporations that hold your and your patients' critical information hostage in a data prison.

Solution: Use or switch to Electronic Dental Record (EDR) vendors that ensure interoperability of your patients' data while also allowing for connections to any software vendor and the ability to bring in data from the vast network of medical Health Information Exchanges (mHIE).

In 2022, a Netflix subscription cost $6.99 per month. In the same year, Netflix invested $18 billion dollars on the content that you paid less than $7 dollars a month to consume. This means Netflix spent 214,285,714 times your annual investment on the product that they sold to you.

Netflix also generated between $5 and $6 billion in annual operating profit in 2022.

Not a bad business, right? Plus they are providing a phenomenal service. Everyone loves getting that $18 billion dollars of content every year for less than most spend on a single dinner for their family.

So how much do you think Netflix would cost if it were the largest software system that was sold solely to dentists through a common, historic company that sells us most of our other non-technological stuff?

To fully conceptualize this idea, let's give it a name.

"Dentflix" sounds about right.

I think it is reasonable to estimate that "Dentflix" would cost well over $100 per month. Probably many times more than that. In fact, one of the largest companies in dental software could absolutely generate a cash volcano if they could dupe dentists into buying some archaic, decades-old software, not unlike our fictional concept Dentflix, for around $500 per month.

Of course, the company behind "Dentflix" would rather stop investing in the content and platform once they achieved a large industry presence, as they have no real motivation to spend their cash here.

There is little incentive for this company to invest in updating their technology, as they own the market and believe that dentists will buy any crappy software, if they sell it hard enough.

Their idea of "investing" in Dentflix typically involves marketing an aging product while trying to protect their fiefdom or chasing markets outside of the traditional dental practice. If they do invest in a new platform, the purpose is to create a more expensive system that serves as a more effective prison for your and your patients' data (more on this later).

It is easy to make excuses for this company and write off this disparity in costs and investment because video streaming is a completely different business vertical from dentistry.

But, let's face it—we all know that there exists something that I like to call "the dentist tax."

The dentist tax is the premium that dental practices have to pay to get the products, services and technology used in dentistry. The same products and services tend to cost much less in other industries.

DENTAL DISORDER

When asked which services have the largest "dental tax," most people mention dental supplies. I do not believe that dental supply costs are the biggest offender, however. Dental materials require an enormous level of quality control and development specifically to tailor these products for our market and that demands a higher cost than something sold to a consumer.

Sure, the cost of cotton rolls may be more expensive from a dental distributor than from Costco, but what percentage of our expenses actually goes into these relatively low-cost products? The total costs of all dental materials and office supplies typically make up less than 5% of a practice's expenses. Once you subtract the cost of true dental materials (adhesives, resin, etc.), you're left with just a tiny fraction of all costs incurred in an average dental practice. Also, there really is not a large variable in cost from one dental supply company to another in regards to the price of something like a package of cotton rolls.

We certainly cannot overlook the impact that the efficacy of products like resins and adhesives have on our ability to produce quality dental care. Spending a little more on such products can often directly lead to higher quality care.

In other words, while dental supplies are expensive, there clearly are good reasons why.

It is true that the cost of any dental-specific product may have a variance of around 20% between suppliers (including direct, discount and major distributors), but there are good reasons for this variance, as well. For example, the prevalence of selling expired, gray and black market products has been increasing within dentistry, especially with online and discount resellers.

For clarification purposes, here are some definitions:

> **Gray market supplies** are defined as legally branded products that have been sold through unauthorized channels. This would include a product that was packaged for another country that makes its way to the United States for sale. Obviously, these other countries may have different regulations and requirements for sale than we do in the U.S.

> **Black market products**, on the other hand, are stolen or counterfeit goods. The prevalence of black market dental supplies has been silently rising over recent years. Black market products are not regulated at all and are usually made inferiorly (to put it lightly).

DENTAL DISORDER

White Market

- The legal, official, authorized, intended market for sales
- Rules and regulatory compliance

1

Gray Market

- Unsanctioned sales
- Sales not authorized by manufacturer

2

Black Market

- Illegal goods and sales
- Stolen, counterfeit, no regulatory oversight

3

Additionally, a trusted vendor in dentistry often has a level of service that would justify the few extra dollars you pay for the product, not to mention the freebies, rewards plans and discounts that they may give you based on your purchase volume.

As mentioned earlier, however, there is a wide variance in the lower cost items that are not dental-specific. The higher cost could be indicative of a supplier's attempt to capitalize on the convenience of ordering everything from one supplier.

A quick Google search on the cost of porcelain etch yielded a good illustration of the dentist tax. Comparing both trusted and sketchy dental vendors, there is about a 20% variance between them in the cost of porcelain etch. But compare the cheapest dental porcelain etch to a similar etch sold at a home improvement store, and that variance skyrockets with the dental-specific formulation costing an eye-popping 1,779 times more than the latter product.

Of course, there may be reasons for this immense cost disparity that I am not aware of. The etch sold through dental channels may have higher quality control standards, extra development and production costs or some other expenses to the manufacturer or distributor that makes the cost of the syringe—pardon the pun—worth the financial "squeeze."

The real culprit of the dental tax, though, is obvious: the lack of competition, especially in the area of dental innovation.

Said another way, there are a select few companies that "own" our industry, and they have massive incentive to maintain the status quo.

However, there are also so many great dental companies where innovation happens all the time. Think of the progress in CAD/CAM materials, 3D printing, adhesives, orthodontics and implants that have occurred over the last decade. It is incredible!

But you know what's incredible in a bad way? The lack of progress in the software that keeps your practice running from day to day.

Look, maintaining the status quo is what most of us want because it's comfortable. Why go through the hassle of learning a new way to do things (and field the ensuing complaints of our team) unless we truly **have** to?

Well, the simple fact that dental practices do not want to change the way they do things has gradually left us behind every other industry. Very far behind.

It has also created an environment in which a select few companies that constitute an oligopoly have been controlling the dental industry. This situation has persisted for decades, quashing the incentive to produce innovative and less costly software solutions. This is also why there is a lack of innovation in dentistry and how the oligopoly can get away with over-charging for inferior dental software.

Dental software is typically outdated, overly complicated (to put it mildly) and fails to account for the workflow of our teams and the migratory and accessibility needs of our patients.

Have you ever wondered why you need to use so many additional services, have so many logins and pay so many bills just to run your office software effectively? Why can you not get access to patient records that you did not create? Why can you not get a pertinent medical history from a patient's physician?

Why on Earth in the year 2023 can a patient not view their own dental records?

In short, software in dentistry sucks, is not accessible and is expensive due to greedy corporations' information blocking practices that hold your and your patients' critical information hostage in a data prison.

This is the sad state of the dental information and software environment today.

Happily, however, major regulatory changes have already taken place that promise to change things for the better, and I want to share these changes with you so that we can all escape this data prison that we are currently trapped in.

I describe these regulatory changes as "new" because this is likely your first time hearing about them. This is a generous description, however, because I don't want to blame our profession for the general lack of awareness of this regulation.

It really is not new, though, as the Office of the National Coordinate of Health Information (ONC) enacted the 2016 21st Century Cures Act (Cures Act) in, you guessed it, 2016. The Cures Act memorialized several laws that will unlock the doors of our dental data prisons.

A few ways the Cures Act accomplishes this is by ensuring that:

1) Patients have the right to obtain their data from healthcare providers as quickly as possible

2) Electronic health record systems (EHR), which include dental practice management software, allow providers to access the records of patients of other providers, enable providers to connect their system to local health information exchanges and support migration from one system to another from one system to another

3) Software vendors allow their systems to link to a clinical data registry

The Cures Act states that vendors should know that information blocking practices likely interfere with the access, exchange or use of the patients' and practices' data. As we will discuss over the next few chapters, the practice of information blocking creates a cascading mess for all healthcare providers, patients and vendors in health care.

Before we move on, it is important to understand how The Cures Act Final Rule defines these three terms:

- **Access** is the ability or means necessary to make the electronic health information (EHI) available for exchange, use or both
- **Exchange** is the ability for EHI to be transmitted between and among different technologies, systems, platforms or networks; it is inclusive of all forms of transmission, such as bidirectional and network-based transmission
- **Use** is the ability for EHI to be understood and acted upon once accessed or exchanged. "Acted upon" includes the ability to read and write and is also bidirectional.

To illustrate the "bullshiitake" that we put up with from our trusted software vendors today, think for a moment about the electronic health information in your practice now.

What would it take to transfer the entire patient record or migrate to an easier, more secure or more innovative software platform without help from anyone? Could you even access your patient database without begging your software vendor?

When a patient today asks for their dental records to be sent to another dentist, what information could you easily, immediately give them?

As I will illustrate in later chapters, you are legally required to give patients access to

their records pretty much immediately. Their COMPLETE dental records. Today, this is essentially impossible, unless you act on the solutions I will describe in this book, in which case you can accomplish this with just a few clicks.

I will outline the easy solution to make this all possible soon, along with detailing the many ways that these illegal practices are harming your practice and your patients' lives.

In short, the lack of dental electronic health information data access and data exchange (said access and exchange often referred to as 'interoperability') is what is choking innovation, stifling competition and keeping your software confusing to use, impossible to access and painful to pay for.

This lack of interoperability, however, is making a few companies very, very profitable.

To learn how to comply with the 21st Century Cures Act easily go to DentalDisorder.com

4

THE DATA DISORDER

"Knowing and admitting a problem are not the same as solving it. But executing a solution is also the fun part, because the solution save you and gets you moving again."

- Twyla Tharp

Problem: We in dentistry are overly complacent about the workflow restrictions that impede our ability to provide the quality of care our patients deserve and the lifestyle that our team members and we deserve, due primarily to our lack of knowledge of acceptable alternatives.

Solution: Recognize the massive impact that the Dental Disorder and information blocking practices have on our ability to provide the best care to our patients, demand that our software vendors comply with the 2016 Cures Act and the Information Blocking Rule and report any clear offenses to these important regulations.

It is widely known that the first step to solving an issue is admitting you have a problem in the first place. So, allow me to present one simple fictional example that illustrates how the illegal practices of information blocking negatively affect every single dental practice, every day.

The New Patient

Like most dental practices, Cleveland's Smalltown Dental has at least one new patient enter their practice each day. At 10 AM today, that new patient was Mrs. Mable Unable.

As Mrs. Unable walked into Smalltown Dental for the first time, she was greeted by the smiling face of Amy, who has been welcoming patients for the last 15 years behind that same desk.

"We're so glad that you're here, Mable," Amy stated warmly.

"I'm so glad my friend George told me about your practice!" replied Mable. "It's such a nice office and so close to my home. I assume you got all my records from my dentist back in Chicago, right?"

Amy clicked around on her computer and said, "Yes, of course! I've got your last X-rays and when you are due for a cleaning. Could you fill out this intake paperwork, please? We need to update your information."

By "update," Amy really means "we don't have any information regarding your medical or dental history from your last office."

"You said they sent my records from the last office, right?" Mable questioned, "I don't have my list of medications with me and I need to be back at work in an hour, so I am in a bit of a rush."

Amy sighed, having had this conversation multiple times every day for the last 15 years. "We can't see you until we have your paperwork completed," her shining grin morphing into a bitter scowl at a speed that perhaps only an annoyed healthcare professional can produce.

"Alright," Mable muttered as she grabbed the clipboard and plunked down on the couch nearby.

Mable then proceeded to fill out the forms as quickly as she possibly could, scrawling out her details in illegible handwriting and checking "no" to all the medical history questions because, hey, it is faster, she had stuff to do and dentists don't REALLY need to know all that medical information, right?

When Mable finally slid the clipboard back to her, Amy realized she didn't have Mable's insurance card. "Could I make a copy of your insurance information?" Amy asked.

"Argh, I forgot my card. I have the information in my phone, though," Mable said, not even bothering to try masking the irritation she felt.

This senseless, time-wasting dance between patient and dental office team member carried on for a painstaking fifteen minutes, roughly twice the time it takes the dentist at Smalltown Dental to prepare a crown.

Good thing Amy gets paid $35 an hour; this conversation about the new patient's paperwork alone made her $10!

With the paperwork finally completed, Mable was then escorted to the CT scanner for more data collection by Smalltown Dental's rockstar dental assistant, Summer.

"Here at Smalltown, we have a new machine that's so incredible that we can see your whole mouth in 3D!" Summer explained enthusiastically.

"But I think I just had a pano taken at my last office visit…" mused Mable.

"Oh. Well, we can try to get that from your last office, I guess, or at least verify that you are eligible for a new X-ray," Summer said, knowing full well that they most likely wouldn't be able to do either by the time Mable left the office that day.

When Summer brought Mable back to the operatory, Mable stated that her lower right was having some discomfort on *biting. So after consulting with the dentist, Dr. Love, Summer took a periapical radiograph of just that area (while they waited to find out if they "could" take that CT scan).*

After thirty minutes of woefully inadequate data collection, Dr. Love came into the operatory and performed the exam. Within 0.25 seconds of reviewing the PA, it was obvious that Mable's #30, which had previously had a root canal and crown, seemed to be failing. This was confirmed with some percussion testing and by the presence of a small fistula to the buccal of the infected tooth.

"Well, Mable… it looks like your root canal on the lower right is not doing well," Dr. Love gloomily informed her patient. "Do you remember whether the dentist or endodontist who did that root canal said if they noticed any problems when they did the treatment?"

"Oh, that was about five years ago, Dr. Love," Mable said. "I'm sorry; I don't even remember who did the treatment. I've moved twice since then."

Dr. Love then scratched her head and thought for a moment before declaring, "All right, here's what I'll do: I'll refer you to Dr. Endo, the endodontist."

Dr. Love felt this was a great referral, as there was really no way to know what else to do, given the little information she had to work with. She didn't even have a good way to obtain the information she needed.

Besides, getting the information needed in this case would consume hundreds of dollars of Dr. Love's team's time, so she may as well pass the buck over to the specialist, right?

(Side note: we all have been compelled by this tragic reason to send a patient to a skilled specialist. This is known by some as the "CYA" referral.)

Obviously, Dr. Love knows that Dr. Endo will likely plan a retreat, having access to no more information about Mable's case than Dr. Love did. Later, Dr. Endo noticed that the distal canal was filled one millimeter short and concluded that must be the cause of the failed treatment.

And so, poor Mable ends up with endodontic retreatment.

After all, retreatment is better than going straight to an implant, right?

Not in this case.

If either of the dentists in our story had the history of Mable's #30, they would have seen that the prior dentist who did the root canal noticed a fracture line and recommended extraction if the endo failed.

A doomed retreatment. Everybody's time, wasted. And poor Mabel was subjected to needless pain, treatment, inconvenience and expense.

We tolerate many, many horrible restoration failures, treatment planning errors, misdiagnoses and heart-breaking patient outcomes due to our lack of historic patient information.

And it's all because of the Dental Disorder and the information blocking practices of our vendors.

Before we move on, let's analyze the example case above to identify the barriers that prevented the delivery of an acceptable level of quality care. In this painful, costly and all-too-familiar example, both the patient and the dental team were affected by these barriers. In the list below, you'll notice that some of these barriers are more obvious than others. In later chapters, we will discuss the solutions to each and every one of them.

Barriers in this one relatable case:

1.   There was no way for Mable's friend, George, to make a direct referral to Smalltown Dental. Mable had to inform the office why she was referred there and by whom. While this doesn't affect the quality of care, it absolutely diminishes the practice's ability to generate more referrals and increase new patient numbers.

2.   The way we send and receive personal health information, including radiographs, in dentistry is broken (to put it mildly). Most com-

monly printouts of X-rays are sent, most of which are unreadable. Alternatively, original digital X-rays are commonly transferred via unsecure (read: not HIPAA compliant) channels, such as unsecure email attachment.

3. There was no way for Mable to actually access her personal health information, even though this is legally her property. Had she been able to, she could have granted access to each provider she sees, all on her own.

4. There was no feasible way for the prior dental team to even give Mable or Smalltown Dental her information, even if they wanted to.

5. To access any information, Mable would have to walk into her previous dental practice and sign a release form, or request the practice to fax her information over. Why not just send a message to the dentist's beeper while eating some Pop Rocks and listening to some Men at Work on your Sony Walkman? Hello 1989!

6. Speaking of last century: paper and a clipboard for medical and dental histories? For more on the idiocy of using this archaic way to receive patient information, read my last book, *The Patient First Manifesto*. Suffice to say, everyone hates paper. It costs way too much money, it's a massive burden for dental teams and it creates the ideal conditions for miscommunication.

7. Looking up insurance information should be neither the patient's nor the dental team's problem. What a colossal waste of time, talent and money! Insurance data should simply follow the patient, just like any of their common health information. If you don't know how much time your team wastes looking up dental insurance info, just ask them.

8. The medical history in dentistry still has not been Standardized. Why it hasn't yet been Standardized boils down to a lack of leadership in this area (more on that in the next chapter). We are trying to fix this. Patients lie all the time on their medical histories. We know this, but for some reason, we continue to accept it. It is time to correct this by being able to see the crucial information that is available to every physician. This is way too important to not address immediately.

9. The lack of adequate radiographic sharing leads to either delaying treatment or, more commonly, additional unnecessary radiation exposures. In Mable's case we get both, as she rejected the CT scan and a PA was taken that would have been deemed unnecessary, if Dr. Love only had access to the CT scan taken at Mable's last office less than a year ago on which the radiolucency was plainly visible.

10. The lack of dental history blinds us when developing certain treatment plans, as was

the case with Mable's previously-docu-mented fractured #30. We lie to ourselves and say the prior dental history "isn't rel-evant," but if we had the history, it would fundamentally affect our options. At the very least, we would have insight into the proba-bility of treatment successes. This is just one scenario, but it is more common than we realize. Think about the effect these histori-cal factors have on your treatment planning: the age of a restoration, prior orthodontic treatments, periodontal treatment, antibiotic placement efficacy, implant failures, psychi-atric episodes… The list goes on and on.

11. Bonus catastrophe! We don't have to wait long for each and every one of these issues to become problematic again. This problem starts all over again as soon as Mable goes to another practice. The endo office is up next, where the cycle of antiquity continues!

And we have only addressed a single tooth in Mable's mouth so far.

Time will fail me if I attempt to elaborate on her peri-odontal disease, poor occlusion, sleep apnea, etc., etc., etc.…

We could detail seemingly unlimited instances in which the medical and/or dental history of a patient is crucial to adequate treatment planning for our patients.

In short, the fact that we do not have access to this information today forces us to provide inadequate care that is only substandard due to the fact that we allow unethical, monopolistic and, now, illegal information blocking practices to persist.

This is not of our doing. This situation is first and foremost the result of pure, unadulterated stagnation by software companies in dentistry.

But the system is fed by our tolerance of it. Add in a dose of stubborn resistance to change, and here we are, stuck with an unacceptably low level of quality as our shining standard of care.

This is beyond sad. It is infuriating.

If you are a patient or a dental practitioner, this should be enraging. This lack of interoperability leading to blind treatment planning continues on in the futuristic world that we live in.

A dental environment where we have had CAD/CAM same-day crowns for over FORTY YEARS, where we have robots placing implants and where we have AI-written chart notes and 3D-printed houses.

It's in this modern world that you cannot get a patient's medical history from the dentist next door.

Have you ever stopped to wonder why you even need to collect data from the patient in the first place? Oftentimes, a new patient has only recently moved and has seen a dentist within the past year, yet you cannot access all the information from the prior dentist with a simple consent from the patient? Even if the patient hasn't seen a dentist, they may have seen a physician, who likely has a current medical history. Why shouldn't we be able to get that?

We currently discount the importance of collecting the new patient's historical data only because it is an unnecessarily large pain in the ass to obtain, not due to how crucial it actually is to the care we provide. In other words, ignorance and the avoidance of inconvenience have eclipsed quality of care.

Hopefully, we are now at the point in our discussion where, having admitted the problem to ourselves, we can move on to step two.

So, let's discuss another adage. It is commonly said that 90% of solving any issue is identifying the core problem. Well, here we have a good news/bad news situation.

The bad news is that in the case of the dental data prison, our solution actually takes a lot of effort to create, as this requires aligning the profession to the solution and then building it in a way that is relatively easy to implement.

The good news is that most of this work of aligning the profession and building an elegant solution has already been done (this solution may even be complete by the time you read this book). The solution, which is either free or costs less than services you are currently using, requires no changes in workflow for you or your team. We will be discussing these solutions more in upcoming chapters.

In our next chapter, let's discuss how you can profit by implementing this inexpensive (or free!) solution.

5

THE PROFIT DISORDER

"Profit is not an event. It's a habit"
- Mike Michalowicz

Problem: Dentists are often oversold expensive analytic platforms that do not lead to a positive ROI and half-solutions that give partial data, omitting the most important KPIs and metrics, putting their profitability at risk.

Solution: Get clear on the data that is essential to run your practice and use solutions that provide complete access to crucial information that is required to operate your practice effectively without overcharging you directly or indirectly, for features and services that you don't need.

When I was seeing dental patients routinely in my practice, every day would kick off with the morning huddle. This was the crucial ten-minute opportunity to set the stage for a productive day of delivering exceptional patient care.

Prior to the meeting, the team would review yesterday's performance, today's scheduled patients and we would discuss the following items in order:

- "How Did We Do Yesterday?" - this included personal production numbers and positive shout-outs to team members who exemplified our core values
- Daily Log Summary- a review of patient reviews, Same-Day-Service percentage (the amount of services we performed yesterday that were not on the schedule for that day) and pre-appointment percentage (the percentage of patients that left the office with another appointment scheduled)
- "What Are We Doing Today?" - a chance to review today's schedule (sharing only the unknown items, specifically relating to new patients and potential bottlenecks in the schedule along with their potential solutions), voice questions for the dentist and let the dentist express their needs for any particular appointment

We then always ended with an inspirational quote (or a bad joke on Tuesdays). I believe it is always best to start the day on a positive note, before the chaos is unleashed on the average dental practice schedule.

At the bottom of our morning huddle checklist was written this simple statement:

> Exchanging information will help treatment
> proceed smoothly and quickly.
> The more you understand your patients
> and their needs, the better you can
> care for them. The planning you do
> in the huddle will have a
> significant impact on our quality
> and productivity today.

In the research I did to prepare for the writing of this chapter, I reread that line for the first time in years. It dawned on me that the Dental Disorder outlined in this book is really just a large-scale version of what we do in an effective morning huddle. A morning huddle should save you time, increase the confidence in your care, remove barriers to treatment and ultimately make you more profitable, while also simplifying your life and the lives of your team members.

Over the years, after consulting for thousands of dental practices, I have run across many offices that do not perform a morning huddle. When asked why they don't meet with their team in the morning before seeing patients, dentists say either, "it's a waste of time" or "we are too busy."

A great morning huddle takes less than ten minutes, but I would estimate that it allows for a minimum of a 10% increase in production every day in our office.

That extra 10%+ comes from:

1) Identifying issues (like a lab case that has not been returned on time) that we can address prior to the patient coming in

2) Seeing where to place key patients (new patients, emergencies, etc.)

3) Discussing previously planned but unscheduled for patients coming in that day, and whether we can fit them into our schedule to get their needs taken care of before, during or after whatever it is they are coming in for (typically a prophylaxis)

4) Motivating the team, which is intangible, yet incredibly valuable

5) Looking for opportunities to delegate to other team members, such as having assistants or hygienists doing sealants (if your state allows), or having one dentist, who doesn't have a patient at the time, perform a procedure so that another dentist can be freed up to deliver a larger case

Again, this is just a sampling of the many, many opportunities and barriers that you can capture in a quick huddle. However, it does require a little focus, leadership and consistency to dedicate to this task every day.

Your team may complain that they need to come in twenty minutes earlier or stay later to prepare for the meeting, so someone has to communicate the value to them. Or it may be you, the dentist, who wants to stay at home with your kids up to the very last minute, so you want to just show up and start drilling.

As Alexander Graham Bell so accurately stated, "Before anything else, preparation is the key to success."

We all know we need to have a complete dataset in order to make an accurate diagnosis and that an accurate diagnosis is key to providing great treatment. This treatment then produces revenue, whereby we pay expenses and, hopefully, have some profit left over to reinvest in our practices. Each one of these steps is required to produce quality results.

Provided it is functioning well, a virtuous cycle is created that allows you to deliver better care every day for your patients.

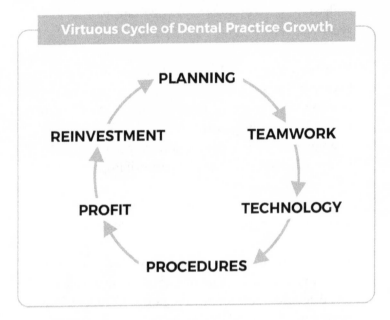

Virtuous Cycle of Dental Practice Growth

PLANNING

TEAMWORK

TECHNOLOGY

PROCEDURES

PROFIT

REINVESTMENT

Unfortunately, it can become a downward spiral if you neglect any aspect of this care delivery wheel. For example, if you are not profitable, you cannot reinvest in your team and your business such that you cannot see more patients, do higher quality procedures and keep the flywheel of a successful dental practice spinning.

Sadly, my dental practice became the perfect example of this downward spiral shortly after I sold it and stopped leading the team. The office manager was replaced, the morning huddle abandoned and our production and profitability tanked.

You know what skyrocketed, though? Our patient attrition rates.

It sounds so simple, but it is true. Once the morning huddle was reinstated and the lethargic practice of ignoring it was no longer tolerated, our production and profitability quickly resumed.

Planning, teamwork, technology, procedures and reinvestment are what lead to profits and positive experiences for your patients and team members.

This is all quantifiable. In the words of one of my mentors, "the numbers tell a story." The numbers of your practice (production, expenses, profit, payroll, etc.) ultimately tell the story of how well you are caring for your patients. While the numbers don't tell the whole story, they certainly at least provide a good summary of your practice's overall health.

If you dig deeper, you will find that by monitoring some high-level numbers, you can determine that it requires just a few metrics to keep an eye on the quality (in addition to the quantity) of dental care you are providing to patients, as well as the quality of both your patients' and team members' experiences.

If your practice provides high-level treatments, such as implants, orthodontics or complex smile restoration, those treatments produce higher revenue. Similarly, if you are helping a larger volume of patients with simpler procedures, like sealants, fillings or fluoride treatments, the larger numbers of your practice will typically reflect this, too.

There are several key metrics, however, that a large part of the profession ignores. A great example of a number that far too few dental practices track is Net New Patients. Yes, most practices track their New Patient numbers, or patients coming into their practice for the first time, yet most do not track how many have quietly left their practice.

So, in the case of Net New Patients we need to start with the number of patients that come to your office for the first time. From this, subtract the number of patients that have left your practice, either because they have actively removed themselves from your records, or because they have not been seen in over 18 months. Lastly, add into the equation your recaptured patients: Patients who have not been to your office in over 18 months, but who now have scheduled appointments.

Therefore, the formula for Net New Patients is:

Net New Patients = New Patients - Lost Patients + Recaptured Patients

If your practice delivers exceptional patient experiences, your Net New Patients number will inevitably grow each and every month. As I mentioned, the numbers tell a story and the Net New Patients number speaks volumes about the quality of the patient experience in your practice.

Keep in mind that the quality of the patient experience is separate from the quality of dental care you provide. Obviously, the quality of your care positively affects the patient experience, but there are many other factors that comprise the patient's overall experience, including convenience, timeliness and friendliness.

I find one of the most interesting of all the numbers that is not consistently tracked is profitability. I say this one is "interesting," because the way profit is viewed in our profession is problematic in a couple of vastly different ways, depending on who is managing the practice.

In a privately held, smaller practice, profit is often shockingly overlooked altogether. Sure, production is tracked and focused on, but in most cases, expenses are largely a trailing metric and handled inappropriately. For example, as detailed in the prior chapter, dental supplies are often a focus of cutting costs, yet they make up less than 5% of all expenses of the practice. Therefore, no matter how hard you try to cut your supply bill, it will likely end up saving you less than 0.5% of your expenses.

Meanwhile, the granddaddy of all expenses in the dental practice is labor, typically commanding a full 50% of costs. And yet, few dentists look at their practice and think about how they can unburden their team of duties, thereby reducing the number of team members they need. This simple step can have a large positive impact on the category that makes up half of dental practice expenses.

Spending a few hundred dollars (or even less) on the right technology can free up thousands of dollars' worth of team time every month. These technologies also do these jobs much more efficiently and in a way that is better for everyone involved, including your team.

One underleveraged technology that your team can use to make more money and make their job easier while also performing the task in a much better way is text-to-pay.

At Toothapps, we instituted Toothapps Pay when we realized that 95% of text messages are responded to within three minutes of being received, and that 90% of people prefer text messages over phone calls.[3]

If patients do not pay for their treatment at the time it is performed (which can be difficult to do when dental benefits are involved), texting is the most convenient, fast and secure method to clean up your accounts receivable.

---

[3]   SMS Comparison online, SMS Marketing Statistics 2022 For USA Businesses, Simon Mannheimer, 12/11/22

What gets seen, gets paid.

With 40% of Americans struggling to pay their bills today,[4] it is important to stay on top of your A/R and be in front of people when they are ready to pay.

It costs next to nothing to send a text message to a patient. Contrast this with the cost of paper and postage and the expense incurred when a team member takes the time to mail out those statements.

You or a team member can send out "statements" via text message to all of your patients with just a few clicks. Then, sit back and watch the payments start rolling in. And your billing can be reconciled automatically without the need for someone to balance the books.

Texting payments to your patients, emailing payment requests and having a payment option directly on your website is a complete no-brainer, yet it is not available at most dental practices.

Convenient payment solutions may seem insignificant when compared to the electronic personal health information we have discussed in previous chapters, but it really is a massive barrier to people getting the treatment they need.

---

[4]   Money.com, 40% of Americans Are Struggling To Pay Their Bills Right Now, Adam Hardy, 7/22/22

Combine this with the fact that so many people have trouble paying their bills, and it is no wonder that cost is the top reason people haven't seen a dentist.[5]

Interestingly enough, however, the same people that are avoiding the dentist are still buying cars and new phones. How does that happen?

The answer is that auto manufacturers and phone companies make it convenient and attractive to buy their products. Dentistry needs to evolve to do the same.

We have a tremendous disadvantage in this area due to the Dental Disorder. In dentistry, the software that manages your patients' dental records (remember, the records are the property of your PATIENTS and NOT of the software vendor) also typically handles your billing. While you may have your billing performed taken care of by an outsourced vendor, the accounting ledger comes from your practice management system.

So, the same information blocking practices that keep your vital patient data locked in a prison, also keep your payment information under lock and key.

Have you ever wondered why your practice system doesn't integrate with Quickbooks or other popular

---

[5]   USA Today, Why 30% of Americans haven't been to the dentist since before the pandemic, Katie Wedell, 8/19/22

accounting software? Wouldn't that make all the sense in the world if it could?

Of course, it would.

…unless you were a greedy monopolistic giant trying to maintain control over information that belonged to the dental practice.

In that case, you might allow for "integrations," but only ones that you could monetize in order to fleece smaller software vendors, making them pay to access information that is actually the property of dental patients.

Want to really get your blood boiling? Think about this huge drain on your dental practice: every single software platform that you pay for, individually pays the same "integration tax" to leverage your practice management software data.

(And may I take this opportunity to remind you once again, because I believe this is a mindset shift that we in dentistry need to make ASAP: this is data that is owned by your patients and managed by their treating dental professionals.)

So if you use one platform for paperless forms, one for online payments, one for recall and another for scheduling, you are paying FOUR different fees to use your practice's information.

In the case of one of the largest practice management systems, they don't even charge a percentage of sales to companies. There is a minimum fee charged to each office that costs about four times the price of a Netflix subscription. On top of that, they have a minimum monthly fee for the vendor that is thousands of dollars, so if a vendor does not have several hundred dental practices signed up for their service, they cannot be profitable at all.

Contracts with some vendors explicitly state that vendors are not allowed to disclose this information (or any other details of their crooked agreement) to anyone.

These huge fees, remember, get passed on directly to dental practices and then ultimately onto patients. You are likely paying over one hundred dollars a month (possibly hundreds of dollars a month) so that technology in your office can access your office's data.

This practice is criminal.

And by criminal, I literally mean criminal, as I would argue that it violates information blocking regulation. Even if the practice management software followed the terms of the 21st Century Act (as of which at the time of the writing of this document, the largest vendor and many others do not follow the terms), they still charge what no one in their right mind would deem a "reasonable fee," as required by law.

Even if you are happy paying these fees for some weird reason, the situation can get crazy stupid.

For example, let's say if you have a DSO with 100 offices, and one of them needs a specific software integration. As is the case with some PMS providers out there, let's suppose that your current PMS is incapable of differentiating between practices that use the integration and practices that do not need it. Your PMS provider's solution is to require you to pay for the software for all 100 practices, even if only one of them is actually using the solution.

Therefore, if the integration fee is, let's say $40 per month, that means that if your $99 per month solution requires the patient data in one office in the DSO, you have to pay $4,000 per month for that one "integration."

That $99 solution will need to charge you $4,099 just to break even, all thanks to the Dental Disorder.

To learn more about information blocking, the dental data prisons and how you can free yourself from the dental payment system prison to increase your practice profitability, go to DentalDisorder.com

6

THE PATIENT
DISORDER

*"America's health care system is nei-
ther healthy, caring nor a system."*
                    - Walter Cronkite

Problem: Neither dentists, nor dental patients, have
access to the dental records they are stewards and own,
putting dental practices at risk of both expensive fines
and damage to their reputation.

Solution: Get involved in patient advocacy and leverage dental software platforms that are, or soon will be,
EEDRA compliant.

While writing the previous chapter, my wife entered
my office with an energy of dramatic urgency and
asked, "Can I ask you a dental question for a friend?"

I reluctantly stopped what I was doing and said "sure," knowing that she would not ask if it wasn't an emergency.

As it turns out, our friends' 19-year-old daughter, Kim, was in a college class when a classmate's hand flew into her mouth, smacking her front teeth hard. Kim was in quite a bit of pain, so she took a picture that my wife showed me. In the picture, it looked like there was a horizontal craze line on #8. I gave her a few tips and suggested Kim see a dentist as soon as possible.

The next day, I followed up on this conversation to find out that the dentist Kim saw recommended referral to an endodontist for nonsurgical root canal treatment on tooth #8, followed by internal whitening and full coverage crowns on #8 and 9.

According to the information that I had, this treatment plan seemed rather aggressive for my taste, but man, I wanted to review Kim's full dental records.

My first question that would easily be answered if I had access to Kim's records is why would this dentist need an endo referral to perform a root canal on tooth #8? Is the tooth not fully formed? Is there a root fracture that was not disclosed to me? Maybe the dentist doesn't do endo at all in their office.

Also, internal bleaching for a 19-year-old prior to crowning...

I'm sorry, WTH? I can't even imagine a scenario where this makes sense.

But all I could do was tell Kim to see a couple more dentists to get some more opinions. She did, and—lo and behold—there was no endo, no internal bleaching and no crown recommended at either of the next two dentists Kim saw.

Think about it, though; Kim should have been able to get those opinions without leaving her couch, not having a new set of radiographs taken at each office she went to.

Even on the medical side of health care, patients typically have access to their records through a system like MyChart. These systems ensure that you only have to have diagnostics done once, as any physician can view the images, results and differential diagnosis list created going forward.

When I ask people if they would like a "MyChart" for their dental needs, they commonly are shocked it doesn't already exist.

You already know why this isn't possible. We have the Dental Disorder and the wardens that oversee the data prisons in our practices to thank for this sorry state of things.

The fact that patient care is substantially and fundamentally damaged from this aspect of Dental Disorder is, in my opinion, a public health disaster.

Earlier in this book, I detailed (hopefully with a dose of humor!) the horrible experience that patients have when they end up in the emergency room of hospitals for dental emergencies.

However, as in Kim's story above, I would think you could relay a similar example of this idiotic Dental Disorder resulting in the needless duplication of dental services every day in your practice. If so, this means that in the average practice, at least one patient every single day has dramatically worse care due to the dental data prison.

And the problem is growing.

People are moving more frequently than ever before,[6] changing jobs, looking for second opinions, being referred for collaborative care and, let's face it, changing dental practices in search of a better experience. In all of these situations, access to the patients' historical data is crucially important.

One dataset that is obviously of huge clinical significance is the patient's medical history. However, the

---

[6] Zillow, Millennials Are Moving More Frequently Than Previous Generations, 10/3/19

medical history of the largest practice management system has been completely locked out of their "integration" such that you cannot write back to it.

This remains the case even if you are a software vendor who pays for their highest priced tier of "integration."

That means that no matter how much you pay this company, if you do not use a system that their sketchy warden owns, they will not allow you to legally write back into your patients' medical histories.

Again, it is the PATIENTS' medical histories. And dentists should have access to them.

This also means that it is likely putting millions of patients at risk of having medical events, all because this company believes that if they allowed access to your patients' records, you would not want to use their services and would flee to their "competitors," instead.

Well, they are probably right. You likely wouldn't use their software unless you "had to." Because their software sucks that badly.

What if your patient has a new medication allergy, just had a stroke or heart attack, was recently diagnosed with diabetes or sleep apnea, had major surgery or any number of life-threatening medical issues?

If you controlled the software in your office, would you hide this information?

Frankly, as a dentist, innovator and software developer, I find this practice crossing beyond the realm of "wrong" or "unethical" and into the landscape of "appalling." This particular topic was the impetus for me to develop Toothapps and to write this book.

As discussed previously, legislation such as the Cures Act has been passed to prevent information blocking, so in addition to being immoral, the practice is also illegal.

And now dentists are paying a more direct price for the data prisons they are stuck in, too.

In September of 2022, three separate dental practices paid a collective $135,000 for HIPAA violations regarding patients' right of timely, affordable access to their medical records.

Here are the reported violations for each office:

- One Chicago-based practice had a patient state that she only received a portion of her medical records and got the rest five months later after filing a complaint with OCR.
- The second office, from Georgia, received a complaint that one patient's records came after a year and a $170 copying fee.

- A Las Vegas office was fined because a mother complained that it took eight months and multiple requests to get copies of her and her minor child's protected health information.[7]

Save for the relatively high $170 records fee, I believe that almost any dental practice could unwittingly commit any of these other violations.

It is not your fault. It is a byproduct of Dental Disorder.

Think for a moment: how easy is it for *you* to give a patient their full records on request?

The fact that you cannot access your patients' records can now put you in legal jeopardy and expose you to federal fines.

This is because you are the legal steward of this data, which belongs to your patients. Therefore, you are obligated to provide the data to a patient when they request it.

In order to address this dilemma, Dental Standards Institute is creating the Equitable Electronic Dental Record Access (EEDRA) Standard.

---

[7] Becker's Healthcare, 3 Dental Offices Pay Fines For Potential HIPAA Violations, Giles Bruce, 9/21/22

EEDRA outlines the easy, inexpensive (and likely free) way that patients can access their electronic Personal Dental Data (ePDD). This Standard outlines how patients can control their dental information and grant access to it to providers that they choose to see, or that they have been referred to, without the need to sign consent forms.

To illustrate the importance of EEDRA, let's consider another fictional scenario that's similar to the kind of cases you see in your practice every single day:

Mary was riding the new ebike she got for Christmas, when a truck swerved out of its lane and into hers, sending her flying onto the pavement at 25 miles per hour.

Mary's helmet protected her brain, but not #9, unfortunately, which broke right at the level of her gingiva as soon as her face contacted the ground.

Badly shaken, Mary traded insurance information with the driver of the offending F-150 and then wasted no time calling her dentist, Dr. Schwinn.

"My front tooth is gone!" Mary sobbed into the phone.

Luckily, Dr. Schwinn uses Toothapps, so Mary was able to send over a quick picture of the tooth. Dr. Schwinn wanted Mary to be seen today, but because he was not in the office, Dr. Schwinn referred Mary to the endodontist who practiced in the same building, Dr. Trek.

Problem is, Mary hasn't seen this endodontist before. So how is Dr. Trek going to obtain Mary's medical history, dental history and the picture that Mary just sent to Dr. Schwinn?

And after the endodontist determines that Mary's #9 can be saved with endo, extrusion at the ortho office and a post, core and crown, how is all of the treatment going to be coordinated?

Today, the real world version of this scenario would be a complete mess, much like the story we discussed in Chapter 1.

Because of the work we have accomplished through Standard development and innovation, however, this case can actually be completed with ease. All it would take are a few clicks on either Mary's or one of the dentists' Toothapps accounts.

As a general dentist, just picture all the communication difficulties you would have to deal with trying to manage Mary's dental trauma. In addition to one or more evaluations, you're looking at endodontic referrals, orthodontic referrals, and possibly even a referral for a medical consultation to ensure no additional damage was done to Mary's face.

Each and every care provider involved in this case will obtain new information that probably won't otherwise be shared with the other providers. And yet, every single piece of information they individually gather will impact the care rendered by the other providers in some way, illustrating how vital it is for the professionals to communicate their findings to one another.

To ensure effective communication, there cannot be just one person who has control of this transfer of data. It is each provider's responsibility to share their results, and at the very least, the patient should have insight into a summary of the treatment that was provided.

Think about it: why should a patient have to sign a consent form to access their own information? We can send their information to other providers without their consent. It actually makes more sense for the patient to have visibility into their care, as well as the ability to control who has access to their information.

Of course the reimagining of how dental data flows will need careful design and will likely need to be modified as we learn more and as further developments emerge. I fully understand that empowering patients to control their information comes with externalities that will need to be managed.

However, I don't believe you can deny the reality that the subset of information contained within the practice management system that belongs to patients should be accessible by patients.

Here is another dilemma that needs to be addressed when we unlock the bars to the dental data prisons:

what information does each provider actually want to have access to?

For example, if you are a general physician, you likely do not want to know every periodontal probing depth for Mary. That would simply be too much information for you to sift through.

Or if you are a general dentist, then you don't need to know about the hemorrhoid Mary had a decade ago in order to treat her periodontal disease.

Everyone wishes they could access all of the information…until they get it all and realize that it is just too much. An excess of unnecessary information could even distract from the details that are truly essential to providing quality care. Clearly, we need information to be pertinent and actionable.

Prioritizing the information on behalf of patients, healthcare and dental care providers is key to optimizing the patient experience and clinical quality.

To help address this issue within the ODIN Standard, we also define what information is necessary to send to each provider every time a referral is made.

Additionally, we will later need to determine which information within the Electronic Dental Record (EDR) and other affiliated software is owned by the patient versus what is owned by the dental practice and what is owned by the software vendor.

For example, at this point I would argue the patient's name and dental history are part of the data owned by the patient, and that notes made outside of the of the official clinical notes are the property of the dental practice. Any manipulation of the data that is generated through your use of the platform (metrics like case acceptance numbers) would be owned by the software vendor, fair and square.

On that last point, I'd like to clarify that this doesn't mean the vendor could block access to that data whenever you want, nor that another system cannot recreate this information that is the dental practice's or the patients'.

All of this groundbreaking (as yet undefined) work is going on currently within the Standard Development Organizations of the ADA and DSI.

If you would like to get involved in the important work of Standard development, find out more at DentalDisorder.com

7

THE TEAM DISORDER

"I can do things you cannot, you can do things I cannot; together we can do great things."

- *Mother Teresa*

Problem: Dental continuing education continues to be largely based on the archaic practice of flying across the country, sitting in a poorly lit hotel conference hall and listening to someone speak at you for ninety minutes. We are all busier than ever and don't want to spend the time, energy and money to consume our CE this way.

Solution: Seek out convenient, inexpensive, on-demand alternatives to get great dental continuing education efficiently via channels like Upgrade Dental.

DENTAL DISORDER

I like to say that it is a dental practice's busyness that typically is the downfall of the business. The true barrier that prevents the average dental practice from reaching the heights of success is the tendency to focus on what is urgent at the expense of that which is most important.

This is so easy to do and extremely difficult to avoid.

Basically, our teams are so overwhelmed with the day-to-day tasks that we cannot stop and think about how to improve what we do in order to free up more time to devote to that which is truly going to help us achieve our goals.

There are shockingly very few dental teams that get their training together. It is shockingly uncommon how few and how infrequently dental teams get training together. I can't tell you how many lectures I have given where there were less than a handful of team members present and (wouldn't it figure) the lecture I am giving is all about teamwork!

While others may equate a dental team to a "family," I prefer to compare a high-performance dental team to a sports team looking to win a championship.

Families typically contain dysfunctional members that can barely have dinner together without an argument ensuing.

Champion sports teams, however, are made up of high-performing individuals who work together to achieve great things.

I would rather work with champions. And **champion teams train together**.

In what bizarre world would just the coach of a winning team get trained?

Or how about we just send the quarterback out to get some knowledge, because we don't want to invest in the other team members?

Hey, our quarterback is our real MVP, so why don't we just send him to the OTA offseason training event. Why bother investing in the rest of the team members?

(Hint: OTA stands for Organized TEAM Activities…)

See? It just doesn't make sense.

At the very least, knowledge and training received by one team member should be disseminated to everyone on the team, but most dentists don't have the bandwidth or interest needed to train their teams themselves

So why don't we train together more often? The answer is simple: training teams in dentistry is just too damn expensive and inconvenient.

Here are the typical ways that the average dental team gets continuing education today:

1) "Free" trainings offered by a supplier or distributor
2) In-person training via a lecture or lecture series
3) In-person training at a continuing education center
4) Online video training

Let's break each of these down individually.

1. Free trainings by a supplier or distributor

Many dental companies provide free training, and this works out very well in many instances. If you want to start placing implants in your practice, for instance, implant manufacturers have a vested interest in training you and your team so that they can sell you their implants. Offering such educational opportunities is a win-win all around, and there is nothing fundamentally wrong with this.

In my opinion, the problem is when the funding of this training is not transparent. For example, there are companies that sponsor courses or even provide a revenue share agreement with speakers, and these little tiny details are buried in 4-point font at the beginning of the speaker's presentation or go undisclosed altogether.

At the end of the day, SOMEONE is funding this "free" training. Just make sure you did deep enough to understand who it is.

If you just bought a $200,000 piece of equipment, then this individual was probably you.

If the training you receive is part of an introduction to the $200,000 piece of equipment, it is likely funded by the manufacturer or distributor that wants to sell you that equipment.

I have lectured hundreds (maybe thousands) of times. I have not once been asked by an audience member "who paid for you to be here?"

Admittedly, it is rather obvious today, as I typically own the majority of a company in the space I am lecturing on, but that has not always been the case.

I know consultants, lecturers and "industry leaders" who love selling you high-dollar items because they get a percentage of the sales, but do not disclose this when they are providing their training. In some cases, they may even charge you for their consulting services in addition to getting paid by the products they sell you on the backend of their training.

So, if the answer is not obvious, don't hesitate to ask, *"do you get paid if I buy this?"*

As the saying goes, there is no such thing as a free lunch.

I know consultants who make 100% of their revenue from revenue shares of products they push on their clients.

At Upgrade Dental, we provide a ton of free continuing education. But it is focused on content for more novice dentists as I want to help out struggling dentists as much as I can. So I personally pay for the free education Upgrade Dental provides by editing, hosting and promoting this content. Many Upgrade Dental Faculty members also create content at no charge and provide their time as a gift to beginning dentists, too. In some cases we have sponsored events, but we always make it clear that the event is "sponsored by" those companies.

Unfortunately, many "experts" lack the integrity to disclose the companies that pay them to sell you stuff.

For anyone who wants to level up beyond the more elementary aspects of dentistry, they can either purchase premium courses or join the Upgrade VIP Membership, both of which are 100% unsponsored, as I find it important to be unbiased.

As with all the products we create, my goal is to keep prices transparent and to deliver 10x the value of the cost.

Again, free training can be great, just consider carefully why it is free in the first place.

2. In-person training via a lecture or lecture series

Man, I have flown thousands and thousands of miles to attend and provide lectures to others in person. So much so that I refuse to even attempt to estimate the time, energy and money it has cost.

I would not have done it any other way, however, as I believe that in person events are one of the best ways to gain information. There is really nothing that compares to attending in person when learning. Oftentimes, I learn more from the attendees at a meeting, seminar or convention than I do from the actual presentation that was part of the event.

The fact that in-person training is effective is tempered, however, by the harsh reality that we are all so busy every day. It is no longer simply impractical anymore to expect dental professionals to obtain the continuing education they need by taking time off of work and spending the time and money to attend an in-person lecture; it is downright impossible.

I would recommend to any dental professional reading this book to certainly go to live in-person events, but I also strongly recommend prioritizing the most important and interesting ones instead of trying to attend them all.

In-person CE events provide the perfect opportunity to travel to new places and to gain experience. This is especially true for clinical hands-on courses, such as placing implants for the first time.

3. In-person training at a continuing education center

Obtaining your in person training at a dental continuing education center affords the same benefits and issues as any other in-person training.

I would like to point out a couple items that are unique to these organizations, however.

On the positive side, selecting a single location to get much of your education can be extremely convenient and fun because you can get to know the educators and other professionals that attend the CE at the center. Many dental professionals I know have made some of their best friends by being part of a continuing education group.

On the other hand, these organizations are incentivized to drag out the content in a way that requires professionals to go through extraordinarily long course curriculums so that they can keep charging for content that really is not that difficult to master.

As one of my mentors, Dan Sullivan, says of his own training courses, "a training center's favorite student is a slow learner with a large bank account."

So if you are a slow learner and have the time and money, live training at a CE center is a great way to go.

But if you want the most efficient, cost-effective way to get your CE credits, there is no doubt that online training for the bulk of your education is the way to go.

4. Online video training

During the pandemic shutdown of 2020–2021, in-person training was impossible to obtain, there were no trade shows and dental procedures came to a screeching halt.

It was at this time that many people learned a new verb that described both a way of communication and the company that created it: Zoom.

Everyone loves to hate video conferencing. But it is undeniable how effective this tool can be. The key to great video conferencing meetings, I have found, is to not treat them the same way you would in-person meetings. It is a different medium, so it requires alternate ways to communicate, similar to the adjustments we need to make when communicating through texting, phone calls or emails.

The same is true with online continuing education.

Unfortunately, most training systems haven't figured this out yet.

Almost everyone I know in dental continuing education couldn't wait to get back to lecturing in person. It makes sense, as that is what they've done forever and they lecture because they love it!

However, as someone who is not just a continuing education provider (I've hosted some major in-person events, like our popular Get It Done Days that have always sold out), but also a consumer of all types of education, I LOVE online training.

As I mentioned above, it is the most efficient, cost-effective way to get most of the training you need.

…as long as the providers of the training know how to deliver the content, that is.

This is where Upgrade Dental comes in.

During the shutdown, I had several large companies come to me asking how they could educate their audiences about new products that they were launching. Given my team's expertise in video production and digital marketing, we launched four products for companies during the shutdown, and every single one of them wanted to do more. Over the next year, Upgrade

Dental became the fastest-growing online dental CE platform, getting over 2,000 registrations to our free Upgrade Day event.

Today, Upgrade Dental is squarely focused on providing the highest quality online dental education for growth-minded dental professionals who want to train together.

Whether your goal is to exponentially increase your production through the popular Insanely Productive Dentist 16-week course, learn to place implants, or train a new assistant, Upgrade Dental has you covered with straight-to-the-point modules that give you the knowledge you need without any of the fluff.

How you choose to obtain your education is very personal. There are tons of fantastic CE providers throughout the dental industry, and I think the reason why there are so many is that each of us is looking for something different.

I talked about my frustrations with how others may view dental continuing education in my last book, *The Patient First Manifesto*, lamenting how dentists will go to course after course to learn more about bonding agents, when all they really need to do is follow the instructions on the package of the bonding agent they use. They would rather validate their knowledge of something that they learned in dental school than change it to be better tomorrow than it was yesterday.

I realize that some people love hearing the same information over and over again. Some people truly don't want to learn new procedures or experience a massive mindset shift that takes their career in a new direct direction.

The majority of dental professionals are too busy to be bothered to look for a better way to practice.

If that is you, fine. Upgrade Dental probably isn't the training you are looking for.

However, if you and your team thrive on progress and want to get the most concentrated information on how to grow your practice, then Upgrade Dental is exactly right for you.

To learn more about Upgrade Dental and how to become an Insanely Productive Dentist, go to dentaldisorder.com

8

THE OWNER DISORDER

*"Build your own dreams, or someone
else will hire you to build theirs."*
- *Farrah Gray*

Problem: There is a common perception that dentists who don't own their practice are massively losing out financially, which conflicts with the persistent belief that dentists are "bad at business" because we did not get business training in dental school or that we are not well-suited to run a business.

Solution: Realize that most people who are involved in business are "bad at business," even the ones that are running huge Dental Service Organizations (DSOs) and, armed with this knowledge, navigate a path for your career that makes the most sense for you.

When you think of the terms "successful business owner" or "entrepreneur" who pops into your mind?

What background and experiences would you associate with successful business owners, managers and operators?

Chances are, you did not imagine the average independent dentist or practice owner.

Consider, though, that the typical independent dentist invests around $500,000 to start their practice[8] and has a profitability of somewhere between 30% and 40%, depending on the source you consult.

Now compare that with the fact that the average small business owner in the US invests between $30,000 and $40,000 to get started,[9] with the average small business profitability rolling in at a whopping 7-10%.[10]

---

[8] The Real Cost of Owning a Dental Practice, ADA Marketplace Online

[9] Annie Pilon, How Much Does It Cost to Start a Business, Small Business Trends, Jan 2022

[10] Tim Parker, What's a Good Profit Margin for a New Business?, Investopedia, Oct 2022

Additionally, the average dental practice has over $940,000 in revenue, while the average small business generates significantly less than half that amount.[11,12]

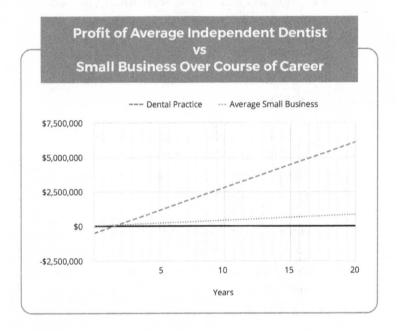

So why is it that in a world where the average dentist takes on ten times the investment risk (not even factoring in the investment of time, energy and health degradation that it takes to become a dentist) generates ten times the revenue and makes almost ten times

[11] Adan Hoeksema, How Much do Dentists Make if They Own Their Own Practice?, Projection Hub, Dec, 2021

[12] Nina Godlewski, Small Business Revenue Statistics: Annual Sales and Earnings, Fundera, Jan 23

the income, that dentists are portrayed as being poor at managing their businesses?

The answer, in my opinion, is fairly simple: we dentists are so busy taking care of patients and our teams that most of us do not schedule the time to focus on our business.

Outsiders tend to perceive our busyness as ignorance.

As I like to say, "busy is the new stupid."

This misconception of what it takes to be a successful business owner is not limited to dentistry, however. When we think of successful business owners, often we imagine someone who has graduated from a prestigious university, has had a ton of business education and maybe even came from a wealthy family, but this is typically not the case.

To dismantle the idea of what the common view is of how one becomes a successful business owner, allow me to describe the life of the number one, still living, successful American entrepreneur.[13]

This industry titan was born in 1954 to an unmarried teenage mother in a small town in rural Mississippi. As a child, this entrepreneur worked as a housemaid and lived a harsh existence growing up, including wearing

---

[13] Marshall Hargrave, Top 5 Most Successful American Entrepreneurs, Investopedia November 05, 2022

potato sacks for clothing and being assaulted repeatedly, both physically and sexually, starting at the age of nine.

Despite these hardships, she found solace in education, reading books voraciously and obtaining knowledge at every opportunity. This future business leader felt validated for the first time when she read Maya Angelou's autobiography, *I Know Why the Caged Bird Sings.*

Possessing an incredibly intelligent sense of curiosity and imagination, this person pursued a degree in Speech Communications and Performing Arts at Tennessee State University, but left one credit short of graduating to pursue a career (returning twelve years later to complete the degree).

Eventually, her talent and obvious charisma caught the attention of those around her and she landed a job as a news anchor in Nashville. She later became the first African American woman to co-anchor the news in Baltimore, Maryland.

Obviously, this number one successful entrepreneur is none other than Oprah Winfrey, who went on to create *The Oprah Winfrey Show*, star in *The Color Purple*, create Harpo Productions and *O, The Oprah Magazine* and start up her own book club and television network.

Oprah is not alone. Many business tycoons, including Richard Branson, Steve Jobs, Coco Chanel and even one of the most savvy business operations minds who created IKEA, Ingvar Kamprad, had no business training prior to starting their empires.

In dentistry, however, many of us look up at the leaders of large corporations in our industry as if they possess some secret knowledge we lowly common folk do not.

Allow me to let you in on a secret:

The leaders of these large companies in dentistry are no better at business than you.

These C-suite executives and middle managers have no special skills that the average dentist owner lacks; it's just that they are actively playing the game of business, while many dentists try to ignore the business aspects of their practice.

Hopefully, you find it empowering to realize that there is no secret sauce that DSOs and other large corporations in dentistry have that we owner dentists do not.

Let's take a moment to discuss a few categories of organizations and "business people" in dentistry, the myths associated with them and the reality that you can benefit from:

Dental Service Organizations (DSOs), Dental Practice Organizations (DPOs) and every other

group of "independent" dental practices that are not owner operated.

I have purposefully lumped into this category every group of dental practices that is not owned by a small group of dentists under the overarching umbrella term of "DSO" because there is an abundance of dental groups forming these days that specifically declare that they are "not a DSO," as if there is something inherently dirty or corrupt about DSOs. These groups often claim that their group is superior to a traditional DSO in some way, typically asserting that their doctors have more control or ownership.

I'm not saying there are not diverse approaches and business models in the dental group space. It's been accurately stated, "if you've seen one DSO, you've seen one DSO." Just as no two dental practices are alike, so it goes with dental groups.

However, I have talked to innumerable leaders of new dental groups who try to position their group as an "anti-DSO" model that will keep dentists in control, only to later discover that in reality, they just don't want to fund the full acquisition of dental practices up front.

Keep in mind that there are groups that both maintain dentist autonomy and allow for asymmetric upside for dentist ownership.

Many times, the "non–DSO" DSOs are just starting out. It could be a consultant starting a group, or even a dentist, who sells the dream of financial upside without losing control. In this scenario, I would advise the selling dentist(s) to think forward a few years, as dental groups typically re-capitalize (or change ownership) every several years, and make sure that you are OK with anyone else owning the practice portion you are selling.

In my personal experience (and in those of many dentists I have talked to), dentists are sold something very different from the reality of what occurs after a sale.

So my advice is, "seller beware."

Getting back to the main topic of this chapter, let's discuss the business acumen of the people working within the dental group organization. There is a common theme in dentistry that the people running a DSO understand the business side of dentistry better than dentists. As is often the case, this is only part of the truth.

It is true that there are many people, in some cases hundreds of people, whose sole responsibility is to focus on one aspect of the business of the dental practices. DSOs, therefore, are able to maintain a large focus on the business of running dental practices.

In many cases, unfortunately, this really just means finding ways to cut costs.

From what I've observed, however, the average person working on the business side of a dental organization is no more (or less) capable of running a business than the average dentist who takes their time to focus on their business. It's just that this isn't a primary focus for most dentists. Arguably, it really should not be the primary focus of most dentists, as our fundamental job is to provide the best clinical care possible.

If you are a dental professional who enjoys the business side of dentistry, however, I would encourage you to not listen to the naysayers. I believe that dentists are perfectly capable of running large businesses. Like anyone else, they just need a great team.

That last paragraph was my attempt to be polite.

Here is my unfiltered experience with the common business people working within a DSO:

The average DSO employee (who doesn't work in the line of care, mind you) shows up to work each day trying to make themselves look good to the CEO or leadership team, regardless of whether what they are doing makes sense or not.

The CEO of a DSO could be someone who leads through intimidation, refusing to listen to others and ignoring facts like they were "Last of Us" fungal infections. Conversely, the CEO could be a great, compassionate leader who truly cares about patients and the DSO's employees.

Whether a DSO is led through intimidation or compassionate leadership depends on the DSO. I've seen quite a bit of both but, unfortunately, I've had more personal experience with the former.

These descriptions (like much of this book) are pointedly accusatory.

So I would like to back up my observations with a couple of examples that anyone with insight into the workings of the average DSO would likely agree with.

My first example is that of the hygiene leader who typically does not see patients, but sells to the DSO leadership team a dream revenue of some new periodontal adjunct, patient product sales, increasing active therapy or skyrocketing scaling and root planing cases.

On the surface, efforts to improve the periodontal health of our patients by any of these means would appear to be a noble pursuit. Oftentimes, however, this is only a thinly veiled attempt to show that if we bring in X product into Y offices, revenue per patient goes up by Z dollars.

While this in itself is also not problematic, I've noticed that these endeavors are always looked at in a silo, completely ignoring how the periodontal adjuncts can affect restorative needs or overall patient care.

We have limited time with our patients and they have limited attention spans, so it is imperative to focus our patient education on the most important aspects of their care, including (but not limited to) periodontal, restorative and cosmetic concerns.

But if you're a hygiene leader who can stand up at the next meeting and say "we sold $100,000 of whitening strips per office," the CEO likely thinks you are a hero, regardless of the efficacy of those strips or the fact that the patient said "yes" to whitening strips at the expense of saying "no" to endodontic treatment.

Obviously, this misdirection of patient education can happen in any practice (and I certainly have been guilty of going down this sad rabbit hole in the past). However, I believe this type of narrow thinking has become institutionalized within many DSOs.

Consider a second area that demonstrates why the average DSO is no better at business than the average dentist: the way DSOs view the incorporation of technology.

Let's use CAD/CAM dentistry as an example and consider how DSOs can grossly miscalculate the value of this technology.

DSO leaders may confidently think, "we have a great contract with our lab, so they only charge us X, which is barely more than a CAD/CAM block."

This is a completely incorrect calculation of the value and cost analysis, however. The cost of the CAD/CAM restoration is significantly more than the cost of the block, as you have to pay for the machine, training, maintenance and upgrades.

The real value of CAD/CAM comes into play in the patient experience.

Undoubtedly, any dentist that has incorporated CAD/CAM into their practice with adequate training would assert that CAD/CAM dentistry has been invaluable to the growth of their practice.

In the case of lab restorations, you have to factor in the cost of multiple patient visits and, more significantly, the overall treatment experience as it is perceived by the patient. Same-day dentistry made possible by CAD/CAM technology is nothing short of transformative, delivering massive value that even some seemingly business-savvy DSOs overlook.

I do believe that associating or partnering with a DSO or selling your practice to one can be a great career choice if you have neither the desire to manage the business aspect of your practice nor the interest in hiring someone else for that role.

I just don't believe DSOs are better at business than dentists; the only difference is that they focus on it more. There is a distinct void of leadership and management acumen in dental care establishments of all shapes and sizes, including independent, group and corporate practices, similar to every other industry.

No matter which level of dental practice appeals to you, rest assured that there are amazing opportunities in every single one of them.

We will discuss DSOs more in Chapter 11, particularly the unfair advantages that they have over the average dentist due to their scale, and what dentists can do about this disparity.

Dental Sales Reps

I have often said, "when I go to hell I am going to be selling to dentists, but not be a dentist myself."

The reason I say this stems from my experience working with some wildly talented and well-educated dental sales representatives whose knowledge is too often discounted simply because they are sales professionals and not dentists.

On just about any topic, from buying cars to investing in stocks, dentists tend to be biased towards the opinions of other dentists. This is clearly seen in every online dental forum that has ever existed. For those working within our industry to support dentists, this bias can be a massive barrier to the transfer of their knowledge to dental teams.

Too often a sales professional's experience is discounted because either the last salesperson sold something to a dentist that did not work for them, or because the dentist only values the opinion of other dentists.

Keep in mind that just as with DSOs, each dental practice and each sales rep is different. I've also observed that the average dental sales professional truly is selling something they believe in and does want the best for the practices (and by extension, the patients) that they serve.

Of course, salespeople are likely biased toward whatever they are selling. They have to be or they wouldn't be selling it in the first place. But what we need to keep in mind is that the sales representative lacks the context of how what they are selling fits (or doesn't fit) into your practice dynamics.

For example, if a rep is selling the latest implant guides for placing superior ceramic implants but you have no desire to place implants in your practice, then that product isn't relevant to you.

But there are much less obvious factors that can come into play.

The sales person might offer something that *could* be relevant to your practice, but the timing just isn't right. There is no way for the salesperson to know this or any other such details regarding how you and your team perform dentistry.

A rep could be selling the best 3D printer in the world, but if your website was designed in 2019 and lacks online payment options and paperless patient forms, fix your website first. The website will bring in more patients and decrease your accounts receivable to the point that it will fund that snazzy 3D printer and free up the time your team needs to complete the necessary training to learn how to use the new equipment.

The 3D printer sales person's quota, however, doesn't include websites.

Like many other dental practice owners, you've probably left that in the hands of some marketing company that charges too much and doesn't have the ability to install the solutions that a modern website should have, including online payments, paperless forms and emergency requests.

The scams of dental marketing companies are another topic that could fill a book. If you want to get a world-class website and practice marketing solutions without getting scammed, you can find those over at dentaldisorder.com.

It is up to those of us that run, manage or work within the dental practice to provide the context by which the sales professional's knowledge is applicable to our practices. Both parties have separate, valuable spheres of knowledge that need to be combined in order to truly determine whether what you are being sold is worth investing in at this time.

Dental Consultants

I am a HUGE believer in coaches. In fact, I do not remember a time in my life that I have not worked with multiple coaches at once. At points in my career, some of these coaches have been dental consultants from whom I have learned immensely valuable information.

A coach or consultant should have some expertise or knowledge that you do not have that is applicable to what you want to achieve. My favorite coaches have already accomplished a greater vision of whatever it is that I want to accomplish at the moment.

When I want to level up my guitar playing, I seek out a great guitarist. If I am looking to improve my painting skills, I look for an artist whose paintings I admire. It just makes sense that wellness coaches should be fit and money managers should be rich.

So when it comes to growing my dental practice, why would I listen to someone that has not grown the kind of dental practice that I aspire to build?

Unfortunately for dentistry, the coaches and consultants in our industry that have owned or managed the kind of dental practice that any dentist would want their practice to resemble are few and far between. They do exist, though, and I would recommend looking for a coach or consultant who has already accomplished what you are looking to achieve.

Dental Software Vendors

In my opinion, there is no aspect of the dental industry that preys on the busyness of dentists and exploits their lack of familiarity with their products more than dental software vendors.

(Admittedly, dental marketing companies are up there on the list too, so let's just say both are quite guilty of taking advantage of dentists.)

When it comes to selling dental software, the largest providers of dental software didn't even develop the software they sell. The largest software vendors in dentistry are usually corporations that purchased a product that was innovative twenty-plus years ago and they are just riding that gravy train as long as they can.

Worse yet, most of the largest software products in dentistry today are sold by companies whose core business thrives when dentistry is kept in the proverbial Stone Ages. These companies often buy into many dental innovation companies just to destroy them.

Disturbingly, these companies that sell the largest software products in dentistry also sell us other things we depend on, like education and equipment, making us helplessly reliant on the data prisons they've built.

In contrast, while the goliaths of Epic and Cerner were forced to allow interoperability to happen in medicine, these companies actually created the software they sell, and they are almost exclusively devoted to software development.

Dentists, however, tend to buy their software from the same company that repairs their equipment, provides them with continuing education and even designs their practices.

Unless our dental community speaks up to demand access to our patients' data for us and our patients, it will not happen soon.

All too often, software in dentistry is developed or owned by companies who are not truly innovative and who are not seeking to improve dental care for patients or help dentists become more profitable.

Fortunately, there are great software companies in our industry that seek to solve the problems choking our practices and who believe in freeing dental practices and their patients from the data prison. To find out who, go to dentaldisorder.com

9

THE IT
DISORDER

*"Out of intense complexities, intense
simplicity emerge."*
                    - Winston Churchill

Problem: Dental practices today usually have only
two absurd options to choose from when it comes
to implementing new technology: hire an IT company that takes too long, charges too much and may
not know what they are doing, or hire someone that
doesn't charge as much, but still takes too long and for
sure doesn't know what they are doing.

Solution: Leverage Connected Dentistry® to inter-
connect all your software applications into an ecosystem of functionality that requires no IT professional to
install or update, but is as easy to use as the applications
we use on our phones every day.

When I sold my dental practices in 2019, my monthly IT bill was over $2,200 per month for just my primary location. This did not include any hardware equipment; just the support and maintenance of our equipment, training, security and backup.

If this seems expensive to you, trust your instincts.

However, while it did cost me almost twice as much as the average monthly home mortgage in the United States of America to protect the integrity of our data and ensure we were up and running at a moment's notice, I didn't really have an acceptable alternative.

Keep in mind that I was (and still am) part of several successful technology companies at the time, so I wasn't spending this money frivolously. And it wasn't because I was paying more than the average dentist would pay for the same services. In fact, I received a significant discount, as I partnered with this IT company in several presentations and had used them for over a decade.

Why, then, did I spend the equivalent (at that time) of 50% of the gross salary of someone in the U.S. on IT support? The answer is because, as we have previously discussed, dental software is typically outdated and there is a significant lack of innovation in the space.

The horrific state of innovation in dentistry was never clearer to me than when I was at one of the best conferences I have attended: Forsyth Dentech 2022 in Boston. At this conference, about twenty-five emerging technology companies presented. Many were looking for investments, collaborators or both.

I went to Forsyth this year because an exciting start-up that I had just started working with, TWICE (a cutting-edge oral wellness company) was presenting there. TWICE crushed it, as did pretty much every other company that was on display. From exciting developments in clinical tech, like regrowing pulp and bone glue that allows for immediate loading of implants, to business functions that show when your sterilizer will fail before it does, I was exposed to some of the greatest minds doing incredible work in dentistry.

I was particularly eager to catch the panel where the Chief Innovation Officer (abbreviated as "CINO") at the largest software company and, I believe, investor in technology in dentistry led a discussion with the CEOs of the companies this software company had recently invested in.

Being in the oral technology space for quite some time, I personally know over half of the panelists that were on this prestigious panel. Sowhen the Chief Innovation Officer asked the first of his two questions to each panelist, I was not surprised when everyone on this panel introduced themselves and their products with intelligence, professionalism and enthusiasm.

What did shock me, however, was the second and last question that this "innovator" asked. Keep in mind that this is probably the highest ranking "Chief Innovator" in dentistry, and someone who gets to determine who gets the most funding to create the next phase of dentistry.

This last question to the panelists started off with a long preamble that circled around how, as CINO, this person has had the honor of working with many different, intelligent innovators in dentistry, who create start-up companies that are looking to build the technology that will elevate the oral wellness of dental patients and productivity of dental practices.

Then the question came. As I did not record it, I will paraphrase it here. While it is not word-for-word correct, it is pretty darn close.

"...Having spent so much time with each of these tech entrepreneurs, I have found that people who create disruptive technology and go through the effort to build a business typically are not well-balanced individuals. In fact, in order to be a successful tech entrepreneur, you have to give up a lot in life. So, one-by-one, please describe what you have had to give up to be where you are today."

This is the one question that the top CINO in dentistry asked of the wickedly intelligent, hard-working oral healthcare tech entrepreneurs, and the very ones whose work he likely funded with a large investment into their companies, no less.

The irony and the threat to dental innovation implicit in this question blew me away.

Frankly, while it is offensive to suggest that successful entrepreneurs are only successful because they have compromised their life in some way, the question also reeks of jealousy. Someone who may have been looking to punch down at people more talented than themself.

Not that tech entrepreneurs are more talented than dentists or anybody else.

Just too talented to be asked this question.

Especially by this guy.

It's akin to having the ability to ask Albert Einstein only one question and choosing to ask him, "why is your hair so messy?"

As I do not possess the grace and composure of these panelists, I would have likely answered his question by stating that I have given up exactly two things to become a successful tech entrepreneur:

1. The ability to perform clinical dentistry on a regular basis and

2. The ability to patiently field moronic questions posed by someone who is in a professional position that they do not understand at a prehistoric company that is trying to make money in innovation when they should stick to shipping cotton rolls (which they are moderately competent at doing).

Instead of the smartass retort I was formulating in my head, each panelist earnestly described, in detail, some aspect of their life that any well-intentioned human being in dentistry could have come up with. From having their jobs keep them up at night to thinking about work while playing with their children, these entrepreneurs gave honest and sincere responses.

In reality, however, there's nothing that you would have to sacrifice while building a dental technology company that you wouldn't have to sacrifice while building a dental practice.

As someone who has built both, I'd even say that building my dental practices required much more compromise in my life than any technology company has. While I don't believe in "work-life balance," I do feel that if you have the drive to be uncommonly successful in any field, it can consume other aspects of your life.

Still, I have never heard someone put a bunch of dentists on a panel and ask them, "what have you given up in your life to be here?" Probably because it is a rude, insulting question to ask anyone.

At the same meeting, but on a different panel, the CEO of another of the top five Practice Management Software companies went on a long diatribe regarding interoperability, in which it was cringe-inducingly obvious that she did not understand what the word interoperability means.

Hopefully, she reads this book.

In fact, both of these companies own many software products that are not interoperable with other solutions they own. I don't even think they have this as a goal.

Their "all-in-one" solutions are really just a means to take as much of your money as possible and provide you with separate products that they purchased that don't work together. Meanwhile, these create significant barriers to your practice and degrade patient care.

This occurs mainly because leaders in the top software companies in dentistry either don't understand innovation and interoperability or don't care about you, your practice and our patients.

Basically, you may end up paying thousands of dollars a month for expensive hardware and an IT company to babysit their archaic software.

This situation may seem dire. Therefore, I would like to present the solution to this dilemma.

As stated in previous chapters, we have arrived at this place where stagnant software solutions act as data prisons because of the anticompetitive, monopolistic and, now, illegal information blocking practices of our trusted vendors.

The solution is to chart a pathway to the opposite dental technology environment; one where secure but open sharing of information exists and competition among vendors thrives. This may scare some, as it seems disruptive. It is, however, quite the opposite.

I'm not proposing that we change our technology in dentistry; we just need to fix it by creating an interoperability exchange that allows every system, no matter how archaic or futuristic, to share data in a way that is Standardized.

Either the software or technology itself will incorporate the most up-to-date technology, or it will connect into a "clearinghouse" style network that will allow it to be part of the solution.

This is what Connected Dentistry® is all about: connecting all our disparate systems within dentistry and connecting dentistry to broader healthcare in a way that anyone can join.

There are good reasons that Apple and Google have constructed entire ecosystems for external vendors to list competitive products that work with their products. Imagine if Apple, instead, had the same policies with iOS and they presented their products iCal, iPhoto and iCloud as the "all-in-one solution" and totally excluded Google services, Microsoft Office and Adobe products because they are competitors to Apple solutions.

This doesn't make sense for Apple because they are an innovation company that develops competitive products. Unfortunately, this is not the case in dentistry.

As someone who has developed several products that require integration into many of the main software vendors in dentistry, I can tell you that their ability to work with others' solutions is, on average, abysmal.

Most dental software vendors rely on what is called an Application Programming Interface (API) to connect their solution into the Practice Management Software. In many cases, these are outdated, don't work with older versions of their software (which thousands of dentists still use) and have known bugs that do not get repaired.

This leads to software companies spending hundreds of thousands of dollars (or more) each year on trying to fix issues that are outside of their control and hiring a team to support the unsupportable issues that these APIs can present.

Dentists, dental professionals, dental innovation companies and our patients deserve better.

10

THE INSURANCE DISORDER

"I used to be sceptic, but not anymore, because now I am positive that I'm getting screwed."

- Dennis Miller

Problem: Patients in the U.S. are not aware that the scam we call "dental insurance" is completely unlike medical insurance. Rather, it's a weak benefit that typically is given from an employer to an employee, and it has weakened even further over the past several decades to the point that it would be comical if it were not harming so many people.

Solution: Empower dental practices, dental patients, physicians and healthcare insurance companies to have access to the same information that the dental "insurance" companies have by enforcing medical-dental interoperability and transparency in reporting.

"I have to say, your clinical dentistry is impressive. I don't think I've seen work this beautiful," said the man sitting across from me.

All that did was piss me off more.

It was about twenty years ago and I was in deliberation with a dental insurance company that was shaking me down for money, stating that the dentistry that I had performed on patients was overly expensive. I had recently purchased a CAD/CAM system and was performing more inlays and onlays than I had previously, and this caused a "red flag" in their systems.

In the words of the insurance company's agent, I "should just be doing amalgams in most of these cases." Of course, the agent was not a dentist.

At one point I was told that I was doing three times the amount of indirect restorations that the average dentist in my area was doing. I was then asked, "what do you think of that? Why do you do so many indirect restorations?" as if I should be ashamed of my work and change the way I do dentistry.

I responded that just as their accolades showed their admiration for my work, I too, was proud of the work I had done. Therefore, I would continue doing the best for my patients as I always have.

Later, I asked my attorney, "Have you seen dentists change the way they treatment plan based on what that moron says?"

To which he sadly replied, "Dr. Laskin, everyone does."

In the end, I settled for very little money, as it was the easy way out. This company was smart; they realized that it was difficult for a solo practitioner to take time away from his practice to fight a legal battle (even if I knew I was 100% in the right). So I just wrote a check and put the ugliness behind me, knowing even at that time it was not the right thing to do.

I have talked to many dentists around this time in Minnesota who were taken for much more than I was.

I also know the brave dentist that eventually took this company to court and won. Turns out he put himself at great financial risk by doing this. Obviously they had many more (and higher priced) attorneys, so his victory was far from guaranteed. But justice in this case won, forcing the insurance company to stop their cruel practice of pressuring dentists to alter their treatment plans at the cost of patient care, simply for the sake of slashing their reimbursement costs.

Insurance companies cannot diagnose or treat patients, but they can put financial pressure on those that do.

In hindsight, I regret my decision to pay them. I should've taken them to court, like the brave dentist I spoke to, as it would've stopped these shakedowns earlier. But I selfishly took the easy path.

While not a direct consequence of the lack of interoperability in dentistry, or of the Dental Disorder, I cannot write a book on the disorder in dentistry and not mention the horrendous business practices I have witnessed dental insurance companies subject our beloved industry to over the years.

In spite of this, during my twenty-plus years of practicing clinical dentistry, I have observed that dental insurance is playing a significant role in the advancement of the quality of dental treatment that our patients receive.

You may now be wondering, "Bryan, have you lost your mind? There has not been one single positive advancement in dental insurance in the last 20 years. Everyone knows this!"

If that is what you're thinking, then you are helping make my point.

You see, the mindset of our patients and their employers regarding dental insurance actually is the massive change that helps patients get the dental care they need. Dental insurance companies have been fleecing everyone in the dental industry SO badly over the last four decades, that no one involved in the industry—patients, vendors, distributors, DSOs and, of course, dentists—believes that dental insurance companies have their "covered" patients' wellness in mind.

This, my friends, is a titanic shift from when I graduated dental school in 1999. Back then, the most common initial question that a patient asked us dentists when we presented treatment was, "does my insurance cover it?" and not "will my insurance pay for it?"

This seemingly subtle patient mindset shift is, in fact, absolutely significant.

This is due to the fact that, just a short two decades ago, our patients believed that their care was covered or not covered based on their dental needs. We dentists would lose our minds every hour presenting treatment to patients, only to have this invisible third party collaborating with the patient to create the crappiest treatment plans known to healthcare.

No longer! Today, dental patients routinely exclaim with pride, "I know dental insurance is garbage," and then ask "why does dental insurance suck so bad?"

When I left the halls of the University of Minnesota Dental School so many moons ago, I had no idea that this is what progress could look like.

Writing a chapter of a book that will mainly be read by dental professionals about the pitfalls of dental insurance could be seen as unnecessary. Preaching to the choir, so to speak.

So in the rest of this chapter, I'm going to point out some new transgressions that dental insurances are guilty of that you may not have been privy to or previously considered. I'm also going to invite you to ponder some solutions (or at least the pathway to the solutions) to this quagmire that we call dental insurance.

Of course, we cannot have a discussion about dental insurance without emphasizing the fact that it is not insurance at all.

The pertinent definitions in the Oxford dictionary of "insurance" include:

1. a practice or arrangement by which a company or government agency provides a guarantee of compensation for specified loss, damage, illness, or death in return for payment of a premium.
    and
2. a thing providing protection against a possible eventuality.

As dental insurance does not guarantee compensation for a specified loss, nor does it provide protection against a possible eventuality, it is not insurance. In other words, dental insurance does not protect against a catastrophic loss, but rather it's a weak benefit that covers some dental procedures to a very limited degree and up to a miniscule maximum annual amount.

Given that everyone—including patients—knows what a racket dental insurance is, why has this farce continued to exist down to this day?

One primary reason is that dentists and group practices have agreed to lower their fee schedules when they sign up to provide services to patients that are part of dental insurance companies' networks.

From dentists' perspective, dental insurance is effectively a marketing plan that they have no control over, costs them a ton, usually has a poor ROI and does nothing to differentiate them from other dentists.

From a patient's perspective, dental insurance is a way to save costs as it is better to have some financial benefit as opposed to none, regardless of how lousy it is.

And from my perspective, I feel that it's time to start referring to "dental insurance" as "dental benefits" in this book as that term has become popular within dentistry (and is far more accurate).

Like most businesses, dental benefits have been impacted greatly by the COVID pandemic. While many medical insurance plans halted collecting premiums during the pandemic shutdown since patients could only get emergency care, dental benefit companies continued to bill patients and employers even in states where it was impossible to get dental care. In some states, dental patients were actually even barred from getting teledentistry services, but they were still billed for their dental benefit plans.

This led to a historical windfall of profits with no expenses. Then coming out of the pandemic, the largest dental benefit companies increased the premiums they charge to patients and cut reimbursements to dentists.

If this were not so damaging to patients, it could be described as comically greedy.

I've been hearing about more and more dental offices dropping participation in dental benefit plans. While this makes all the sense in the world, in terms of maintaining profitability in the dental practice, I do believe that this is going to have a negative impact on patients getting the care that they deserve and need.

In a country where some 50% of adults don't see a dentist regularly, we need to do better for our patients.

Earlier, I promised to point out some possible directions to turn this dental benefit predicament into an opportunity to help dental practices and patients.

First, however, I need to describe how the interplay (or lack of interaction, more accurately) between medical insurance and dental benefits plans makes the often-sought goal of oral-medical integration difficult, if not impossible, to achieve.

Let's start with what would seemingly be an easy and obvious benefit to everyone: acting on the well-known connections between diabetes and periodontal disease.

It has been shown that 95.1% of type 2 diabetic patients have some degree of periodontal destruction.[14] Diabetes has also been shown to be an unequivocal risk factor for periodontitis[15,16] and periodontal disease affects nearly 22% of those with diabetes, making it the most common dental condition affecting those living with the disease.[17]

The obvious conclusion of this information is that all patients with newly diagnosed periodontal disease should be tested to see if they have diabetes, and all

[14] Singh, V Kumar Bains, R Jhingran, R Srivastava, R Madan, S Chandra Maurya, I Rizvi, Prevalence of Periodontal Disease in Type 2 Diabetes Mellitus Patients: A Cross-sectional Study, *Contemporary Clinical Dentistry*, 2019

[15] Salvi GE, Carollo-Bittel B, Lang NP. Effects of diabetes mellitus on periodontal and peri-implant conditions: update on associations and risks. *J Clin Periodontol.* 2008

[16] Khader YS, Dauod AS, El-Qaderi SS, Alkafajei A, Batayha WQ. Periodontal status of diabetics compared with nondiabetics: a meta-analysis. *J Diabetes Complicat.* 2006

[17] What Is The Link Between Diabetes and Periodontal Disease, *MedicalNews Today,* June 2022

diabetic patients should be screened for periodontal disease. While there has been some momentum gaining towards making this clearly beneficial scenario a reality, one simple superficial question is often overlooked:

Who is going to pay for these screenings?

Dental benefits and medical insurance are often provided by different companies, and even if the patient uses the same company for both, the medical insurance and dental benefits plans function completely differently.

Medical insurance is a safety net against a catastrophe, while dental benefits are a weak reimbursement that has a low annual maximum. But if medical insurance were to cover the costs of periodontal screenings as well as the potential periodontal treatment, they would, in theory, reduce the cost of treating diabetes.

There is zero financial incentive, however, for dental benefit companies to cover the costs of screening for diabetes or even participate in solutions that involve screening diabetic patients for periodontal disease because their costs would increase either way.

Additionally, there is no interoperability of data between dental benefits providers and medical insurance providers, so there are technical challenges to overcome in order to provide diabetic and periodontal patients with this level of integrated care.

Herein lies the solution: we must strive for interoperability of medical and dental data and have the ODIN Standard implemented ubiquitously throughout dentistry. In this way, we can at least provide the base level of insight into our dental patients' diagnoses, which would allow for actionable treatment planning in all medical-dental integrative cases.

ODIN has been created specifically with medical-dental interoperability in mind, as there are separate sections devoted to outlining the critical data bundles that a dentist should receive from a medical practice and that a non-dental healthcare provider should receive from a dental practice.

As we have previously discussed, this is vitally important because without defining the critical data elements that should be exchanged, the healthcare professional would be overwhelmed with superfluous information that does not pertain to their scope of practice.

For example, as a dentist, I don't care that you had a wart removed or had your finger stitched six months ago when you had a small accident installing a garbage disposal. And a physician doesn't want to sift through every detail of your dental chart, including each small carious lesion that has been filled, in order to find out that the patient has a necrosing palate.

Therefore, ODIN defines two new narrow data bundles to support the dentist in reviewing medical histories from outside of EDRs and to highlight the elements of the dental history that are important for non-dental professionals in the line of care to know.

These are:

1. **The Dental Medical History Summary (DMHS).** This includes the medical history elements from the USCDI that are covered under the CURES Act that are vital for a dental professional to know about the dental patient (I will explain more about the CURES Act and USCDI in the upcoming chapter "The Cure").

2. **The Dental Specific Summary (DSS) data bundle.** The DSS includes vital dental-specific information that any healthcare provider treating the patient outside of dentistry should be aware of.

We know that the patient's oral wellness is a window into their overall wellness and that there are so many systemic diseases that first present as oral abnormalities. Besides the periodontal-diabetic connection we just considered, oral manifestations have also been linked to obesity, heart disease and autoimmune disease (among many others).

Also, there are conditions that necessitate clear communication between medical and dental providers, such as the areas of sleep dentistry, temporomandibular disorders (TMD) and orofacial pain.

What is also clear is that we need to have our patients' electronic Personal Dental Information (ePDI) and their electronic Personal Health Information (ePHI) from medical providers be interoperable.

Another major aspect of the insurance disorder that we must address at some point: is determining who is ultimately responsible for the overall care of the patient, including both the medical and dental treatment.

Fundamentally, there is no single do-it-all entity responsible for both the dental and medical needs of the patient. We are also entering a new age of patient autonomy, a time in which patients have more say in their medical and dental than ever before. In many cases, patients act as their own advocate in their treatment.

I believe this is an incredibly positive and powerful development that allows us to partner with patients in their care. Therefore, it is essential for patients to have access to their dental records, just as they can already access their medical records.

That is why at Dental Standards Institute we have created the Standard Equitable Electronic Dental Record

Access for Dental Patients, or EEDRA for short. EEDRA allows for dental patients to access their dental records in much the same way that medical patients can get access to their medical records through applications such as MyChart.

The combination of ODIN and EEDRA allows for secure but open accessibility to dental records for dental professionals and patients, respectively, giving those in the direct line of care access to the information they need to deliver and coordinate the highest quality of dental care possible.

Both of these important Standards, along with other Standards that are more acutely focused on dental benefit adjudication and reporting, empower dental patients and professionals.

Being as problematic as it is, should dental benefits go the way of gold foil and be sunsetted to make way for medical insurance that also covers dental care?

While this is an important question, my honest answer is that I have no idea.

The impacts and externalities of this broad solution are beyond my personal scope of knowledge. There are some options, however, that others have been working on to help address the current messy state of dental benefits.

One possible answer to the dental benefit disorder is for more companies to self-insure.

Think about it; the average dental benefit plan costs about $500 annually and has a maximum benefit of around $1,500. So, the potential liability is, at most, $1,000 per employee. Add to this the fact that many patients will never hit their maximum and many won't even use the bare minimum of treatment, and self-insuring makes all the sense in the world.

While dental benefit companies often tout themselves as "non-profit," this is really just a tax status. There are millions, if not billions, of dollars of overhead that dental benefit companies suck out of the entire dental industry.

These days, dental benefit companies are not the only ones that can negotiate a better fee structure from dental practices in exchange for patient referrals.

In addition to self-insured companies that seek out reduced costs, dental discount plans are also growing in popularity. It's becoming increasingly more common for dental offices to offer their own discount plans to patients, primarily for those who do not have dental benefits through their employer. There are also quite a few companies that have developed discount plans that dental practices can easily incorporate.

When it comes to these discount plans, there are some differences between state legislatures, so make sure to check your local laws before developing a discount plan or signing up for one of the many third-party managed plans.

I can tell you from personal experience that creating a discount plan at my practices was massively, positively impactful and profitable. Therefore, while the merging of dental and medical insurance may be an eventuality, self-insuring and dental discount plans are clearly good alternatives to the decaying institution of traditional dental benefits.

To learn more about ODIN, EEDRA and secure, open sharing of ePHI and ePDI between care providers, go to dentaldisorder.com

11

THE DSO DISORDER

"Bigger companies are too cumbersome to move quickly; this can be a competitive advantage for you."
- Sir Richard Branson

Problem: Large group practices like DSOs, have several advantages over independent dental practices which include access to volume discounts on supplies and equipment and the ability to form partnerships with other large organizations that may not have previously worked within the dental industry.

Solution: Dental practices can leverage technology and organizations to achieve the same benefits that are otherwise reserved for large dental groups or benefit from joining the growing trend of participation.

DENTAL DISORDER

On December 31st, 2010, I signed the paperwork and purchased a dental practice that was less than a mile away from my existing dental practice with the goal of merging them together.

If you have purchased one or more dental practices, then you know that the process usually takes several months, if not years, and that there is a tremendous amount of details that go into the planning and execution of the transaction.

In the case of this practice, it took about a year of work. The dentist who owned the practice wanted to sign the documents on New Year's Eve, the last day of the year, so that he could finish the year off as owner before transitioning to being an associate dentist in the newly combined practice.

I was shocked when I received a call from the financing bank the next morning on New Year's Day. Banks are usually closed on New Year's Day, right?

"Dr. Laskin, we need a list of all the equipment from the office that you purchased yesterday," the banker demanded.

I replied, "I don't think you have the right guy; we already closed the transaction."

"I know," the banker answered.

I was a bit bewildered at this point. "Well, sir, that request would have made sense to ask months ago," I started to protest. "Even a week ago I could have gotten you the answer, as a list like that would take several days to produce. But, my friend, you've already lent me the money and I own the practice, so what good does the list do today?"

"I need a list of all the equipment and supplies as quickly as possible," he insisted.

"So if I grab a crayon and take ten seconds to scribble down on a piece of paper some things that are in the practice and send that your way, will that work?" I questioned.

"I just need the list," he replied.

"Are you going to have lots of follow-up questions about this list to verify that what I purchased with the money you already lent me is valid? For example, if I write that the practice I already purchased has a therapy unicorn to combat patient anxiety, are you going to need to ask me what color that unicorn is?" I pondered aloud.

"I just need a list."

While I had him on the phone, I wrote a list on a piece of printer paper that had line items like "chairs" and "pencils" and emailed it directly to him. He then hung up, and I never heard from him or another bank representative about the transaction again.

At this point, I had already purchased a few dental practices, so I was well familiar with the pitfalls that come with buying and selling dental practices. That banker did not stand a chance of wasting my precious time on that first day of 2011. I, on the other hand, now faced the real work of combining the practices into one new location.

Over the next several years, I ended up buying two more practices and developing several technologies.

I sold my dental practices to a large DSO in December of 2018. At this time, OperaDDS, the first technology platform I created, was just starting to take off after several years of development. I needed to exit my practices to free myself up to focus on Opera and the other tech companies that I had created and invested in.

My primary practice was a well-oiled machine that was led by a great management team. I had just purchased a second location and planned on acquiring several more over the next few years with the sole objective of increasing the valuation of my original practice. If this does not make sense to you now, it will in a bit when I explain the "DSO aggregation game."

One of the reasons why there is so much private equity money flowing into the dental industry is because dental practices are basically good businesses (see the chapter "The Owner Disorder"). And as the average dental practice usually suffers a lot of inefficiencies due to its smaller size and a lack of leveraging technology, many firms see the potential that can result if they optimize such practices, primarily by cutting costs. More about this in a bit, too.

But before we move on, let's unpack these two concepts: technology and scale in the dental business.

When it comes to technology, dental practices on the whole are woefully behind companies in other industries. This is a topic that I have been interested in throughout my entire career, as I have such a love of technology and it has been key to my success in dentistry.

I have concluded that the reason dentistry and healthcare in general are so far behind many other industries in incorporating technology into their practices is because healthcare professionals are conservative by nature and very, very busy.

This poses the classic conundrum of having to slow down to learn a new way of doing things in order to speed things up.

And slowing down in a dental practice is very challenging.

I can tell you, however, that the larger a dental organization is, the more people there will be who can take the time to evaluate technology. I recently learned that one DSO has a full-time "app manager" whose sole job is to evaluate all the software applications that are running in the practices and try to bring them into efficient alignment.

Yes, this is a full-time position.

This position does not include evaluating hardware or any clinical technology—just applications such as secure email, intra-office communication, paperless forms, teledentistry, eRx writers, payment solutions, recall, reviews and analytics.

Obviously they were interested in Toothapps, as we bring every application together into one simple, unified, cohesive ecosystem through Connected Dentistry®.

Large dental practice groups do contend with unique challenges, like having to align many systems' information into a unified, normalized system. But fundamentally, all of us face the same obstacles to delivering dental care.

But what DSOs recognize is that dentistry is becoming more consumer-focused. It's become increasingly more important to provide convenient and cost-effective dentistry because that's what patients want.

Also, the automation of many tasks within a dental practice is now a virtual necessity, given how difficult it is these days to find exceptional team members (or even just adequate team members).

Leveraging technology is vital to automating care, improving our patients' experiences and elevating the quality of the care we provide. When it comes to the technology in a dental practice, I do not believe that DSOs have an advantage over individual practices because the biggest barrier to successfully leveraging technology lies in implementing it. This is DSOs' Achilles heel. The more people and practices and teams an organization has, the more bureaucracy they have, and the more difficult it becomes to implement any change.

In a large group of dental practices, just getting people to create a login for a new account is a pain in the butt, no matter how beneficial the new technology may be. Perhaps the Chief Technology Officer is too busy with some team BS or a Regional Manager is so distracted by some other "shiny object" in the organization that it's nearly impossible to get access to the dental practice team that actually wants to get going with some revolutionary technology.

If you are reading this and you work within one of these large organizations, I would suggest you seek out technologies that leverage ODIN and interoperability through the dental Health Information Exchange (dHIE) to provide the answer to this Dental Disorder. Implementation of new applications can then be easily done with just a couple clicks.

If you are an independent dentist, I would implore you to leverage the advantages inherent in your smaller team size and focus on implementing the technologies that help alleviate your team of mundane, laborious tasks and make your practice more convenient for patients.

These steps are so impactful because technology makes it easier to deliver higher quality, more efficient dentistry at higher profits, with fewer wage costs. If you disagree with this last statement, I believe you should do some research here. This is the topic of my first book, *The Patient First Manifesto*, so I won't belabor the point here.

However, I must point out that the ability to invest in and implement technology into archaic practices is a huge opportunity for private equity companies to increase the profitability of the dental practices they buy. Keep in mind, the people that run DSOs are not usually dentists themselves and they often are well aware of the fact that they know next to nothing about dentistry. They just realize that dentists have under leveraged technology in their practices and this provides a phenomenal opportunity to increase profitability.

Now let's move on to the second reason there is so much activity with dental practice aggregation: the benefits of scale.

As you already know, buying in bulk leads to lower prices. What you may not know, however, is how massive the discounts can be. For example, when I was recently touring the manufacturing facility of one of the largest dental manufacturers, I was told that large DSOs paid 75% less for materials than individual dentists.

You read that right…. 75%!

Large group practices have whole teams that use technology specifically devoted to buying stuff (also known as procurement). These teams are focused on securing the lowest prices from distributors, purchasing directly from manufacturers and managing inventory.

There are "buying groups" out there that attempt to pass along some of these savings to individual practices and some do a decent job of this, but DSOs still have an unfair advantage when it comes to buying materials and equipment at scale.

In my opinion, however, the way all of us buy stuff in dentistry needs to be improved. Having to write in a legal pad or scan some silly barcode on a product to manage our expensive dental supplies is quite outdated.

I am scared to think of the thousands and thousands of dollars of inventory that I have wasted paying people to squabble over supply ordering only to end up with expired products, accidental surplus orders and a stash of products that we never even end up using.

At Toothapps, we are addressing this disparity in scale and preventing the leakage of profits in supply ordering by developing Toothapps SIM – Smart Inventory Management. SIM uses Artificial Intelligence (AI) to read chart notes, the practice calendar and billed procedures to create automated ordering of supplies. For the first time, managing inventory and ordering products will be easy, and we will allow ordering from distributors and manufacturers in a way that is equitable for everyone.

But DSOs don't just benefit from the lower pricing on consumables and equipment due to their size. The "big win" in their business plan comes from increasing their valuations as they increase their profits. This is the "DSO aggregation game" that I mentioned earlier. It works because large group practices are bought and sold based on a scalable multiple of EBITDA.

EBITDA is short for earnings before interest, taxes, depreciation and amortization. But, for our purposes here, we can simplify EBITDA as a measure of profitability. So, when evaluating practices for acquisition, DSOs are looking to "purchase EBITDA," essentially buying a practice's ongoing profits.

Where things get really interesting is when you consider the other factor in the DSO aggregation game, the multiplier. Companies that have larger profits, more locations and more diverse business plans tend to have less risk of their EBITDA degrading over time, so they typically command a higher multiple to acquire than organizations with more modest profits.

So while an individual practice can typically be bought for three to seven times EBITDA, a large DSO can command ten, fifteen and sometimes over twenty times EBITDA.

Due to the varying methods that people use to determine dental practice valuations, Toothapps commissioned a study to evaluate how to

estimate the value of any dental practice.

Here is the summary of the study's findings:

Practice Valuation - Multiple of EBITDA

- Solo Practitioner | 3-5 times
- Multi Group Practice | 4-5.5 times
- Multi Doctor, Multi Location | 5-7 times
- Group Practice (3-50 Locations) | 7+
- Corporate Group Practice (50+ Locations) | 10+

*Toothapps Vantage Minnetonka Advanced Professional Studies 2021

To illustrate the DSO aggregation game, here is a simple everyday example that may apply to you.

Let's say you own a practice that has profits of $500,000 per year and you are looking to sell to a large DSO. Well, you have succeeded in creating a great practice with nice EBITDA, and the DSO is willing to purchase your practice for five times EBITDA, or $2.5M.

Not bad, right?

Well, in our example, the DSO that purchases your practice has 100 practices, so their next sale to a private equity firm (which happens every five years or so) will be at ten times EBITDA.

This means that the moment the DSO acquires your practice, they have doubled the value of the practice on their P&L. So any incremental growth of the practice after this date is just gravy.

I want to mention here that I do not disparage DSOs for playing the aggregation game at all. In fact, I think it makes all the sense in the world for this to be happening. And, unlike the insurance dilemma outlined in the previous chapter, DSOs still have a vested interest in creating quality care and patient experiences.

So in my opinion, everyone can win in the DSO aggregation game. But you can't win a game without knowing the rules, which is why I have attempted to outline them here.

Look, even DSOs want dentists to know the rules of the game, as it allows them to acquire higher quality practices. They are using someone else's money to buy these practices, so they would be happy to pay more for better practices that deliver better care, so that they can keep the profits rolling and sell for more in the near future.

But as DSOs grow in size, the problems that arise from the lack of interoperability and the overall Dental Disorder get amplified exponentially across the entire organization. Imagine the challenge of running 100 dental practices that use five different practice management systems, ten different recall systems and a selection of clinical technology that's as diverse as each new practice that joins the group.

Clearly, as dentistry continues to aggregate, Dental Disorder issues will escalate unless we implement interoperability to address them.

If you are a DSO, implement interoperability to instantly see the profitability of any individual practice, estimate the value of every practice, automate procurement and normalize data easily, while obtaining insight into all the important metrics across your entire organization at every level.

If you are an independent dentist, leverage interoperability to easily implement new technology to elevate your care and patient experiences, while also making your practice more valuable to potential acquirers.

12

THE CHANGE
DISORDER

*"Progress is impossible without change,
and those who cannot change their
minds cannot change anything."*
                    - George Bernard Shaw

Problem: Dental practices are busy taking care
of patients every day, so it is difficult to implement
change within their practice, let alone aid in creating
systemic change within the dental industry, no matter
how positively impactful that change may be.

Solution: We in dentistry need to work together
to create lasting, positive change in our profession
because if we fail to do so, others will chart a path that
benefits themselves (and not us or our patients).

The American Dental Association was founded in
1859 when twenty-six dentists met in Niagara Falls,

New York to create a national representative membership of dentists dedicated to promoting high professional standards and scientific research.

Today, the ADA has over 159,000 members.

While dental professionals constantly debate the direction that the ADA takes on any issue at any point in time, what cannot be debated is the impact that the ADA has had on dentistry.

And it all started with a group of people that was smaller than the team size in many dental practices today.

As Margaret Mead said, "Never doubt that a small group of thoughtful, committed citizens can change the world; indeed it's the only thing that ever has."

I believe that we are currently at a crossroads in dentistry. We can either do the light lifting required to address the Dental Disorder and finally have access to the vital information we need to deliver higher quality dental care, unburden our team members and make more money with ease, or we can sit back and allow the large companies that run our industry to run over us and our patients.

To the dental professionals, patients, vendors and industry partners who have read this far, I applaud you. I know how busy you are and that taking time out of your schedule to sit down and read a book (even one as brief and entertaining as this one) is a BIG deal.

But, we have work to do. The Dental Disorder will not solve itself.

In fact, there are some big dental corporations that would benefit from our resisting and delaying the transition to a better future. And, as I have described in both this book and in *The Patient First Manifesto*, creating lasting change in dentistry can be difficult.

Doing something tomorrow differently from how you did it yesterday can often seem scary and overwhelming.

Therefore, explaining how individuals can easily assist in addressing Dental Disorder, along with describing the "size of the prize on the other side of change," as I like to call it, can help move us all to action.

To that end, let's list out some enormously positive aspects that will come to fruition once we address Dental Disorder and work to have open, secure interoperability in dentistry:

1. Better Patient Care

Whenever reviewing any new technology, the first question we need to ask ourselves is, "how does this change affect the quality of dental care our patients receive, as well as our patients' overall dental experience?"

In the case of increasing dental information interoperability, the amount of data we obtain about the patient is directly correlated to the quality of care that we can provide. From more complete medical histories and comprehensive dental histories to original copies of all radiographs and data on perio, endo, ortho, TMD, emergency care and so much more—just think of how much more effective your treatment would be if you and your patient could access everything, even details about seemingly inconsequential aspects of their dental care. This is why I believe that there is no better way to increase the quality of dental care than to address the Dental Disorder.

For example, at first glance, you may not think it's important to have a dental patient's recall information available in an interoperable fashion. But you know that the frequency of visits is important to know, such as if the patient is on a three-month, six-month or annual cleaning schedule.

Think too about the benefits inherent in having all the radiographs and dental records at hand when developing treatment plans and providing care. You will have several angles to evaluate to determine the location of that mesial canal is when doing endo, the last few years of radiographs will help you determine whether that incipient lesion was there two years ago and you will be able to review notes that will help you learn the patient's track record of compliance/adherence in regards to wearing clear aligners before you recommend ortho, again.

These are just the obvious benefits of interoperability recall data. So let's discuss an example of how interoperability will positively transform our quality of care in a way that you may not have considered: recall notifications.

Why on Earth do dentists need to pay $200, $300 or even up to $500 a month just to send a notification to the patient that they have an appointment coming up? Why don't we just send a calendar invite via email and/or text like the patient receives for every other event in their life? We can then let Google, Apple or Microsoft notify the patient in that convenient way that people manage all of their other appointments.

For far too long in dentistry, we have had to create whole new systems to compensate for this artificial barrier by sending recall notices. It costs too much, it is too complicated and, in the end, the patient has little to no control of their appointments.

I believe so strongly in a robust recall system that I created one in OperaDDS that I believe is second to none. When we address Dental Disorder adequately, however, recall systems will be optional.

2. Access to Dental Care – More Convenient Care

I have included two line items here that describe how interoperability will increase accessibility to dental care, as I believe there are two fundamental ways that this important aspect of dental care will be achieved: through more convenient care and lower cost of care.

Accessibility to dental care is one of the primary concerns that our profession needs to address. Accessibility is often the rationality used when new regulations and rules are thrust upon dentistry, such as developing new and more comprehensive roles of auxiliary team members.

This means that if dentistry does not work to expand accessibility to our services, we will continue to be compelled to do so in ways that will benefit neither us nor our patients.

When it comes to providing more convenient care, addressing Dental Disorder will allow patients to more readily access emergency triaging, virtual consults and even active treatment.

From being able to instantly communicate with a dental professional at any time, set up your appointments online, pay your bill from a text and having teledentistry ubiquitously available to patients anywhere, you cannot deny the fact that interoperability will allow for more convenient care.

We could unpack and review in depth any one of these fantastic solutions that leverage interoperability to open up more options for patients to receive better care.

However, I would like to zero in on teledentistry for a bit as it is so commonly misunderstood.

Teledentistry was the hottest new technology in dentistry that I had witnessed in my career. It was national news during the pandemic, and I was on an average of six webinars a day discussing the topic. I was featured on national and local news explaining all the benefits of teledentistry directly to patients.

This went on for about two weeks. Then nobody cared.

I believe this happened because people did not know when and how to integrate the technology of teledentistry into their practice to unlock the benefits, let alone do so profitably.

No, you cannot prep a crown through teledentistry today. But it does make it easy to triage emergencies, provide virtual consultations and, in many cases, treat patients remotely. It could help you follow up on TMD and sleep dentistry appliances, do care calls in cases where a patient may have a high likelihood of post-operative complications or conduct new patient interviews.

If you were the patient, would you want to take time off of work to travel across town and sit in a "waiting room" only to have an auxiliary team member say peer into your mouth for twelve seconds, say "looks good" and then say you can go home now?

No, you wouldn't. But we needlessly make our patients do this all the time.

3. Access to Dental Care - Lower Cost of Care

As interoperability will increase the quality of care, it will simultaneously decrease costs. This will be achieved through the automation and simplification of many tasks that today are handled by our team members.

But, just as there are obvious benefits to the improvements interoperability provides to our quality of care, so it goes with lowering the costs of care.

On the more obvious side, the improved communication would lead to easier ordering of supplies, requiring fewer people to accomplish more and higher quality work.

There are also huge but hidden improvements that lower the cost of care through interoperability.

For example, interoperability will drastically improve collaboration and reduce miscommunications. The number of laboratory remakes will plummet as AI restorative design and virtual treatment planning will become empowered.

Unfortunately, as stated previously, most PMS vendors explicitly limit the information that they integrate with which limits what functionality can be performed, even with their exorbitant fees.

So while you may be spending hundreds or even thousands of dollars today to allow a new, emerging technology to integrate with your PMS, they likely limit any new integrations such that you cannot perform the functions that are required to unlock the benefit of the new solution.

Want to know how much your PMS vendor charges for these integrations and how they limit access to your patients' data? Do yourself, other dentists and your patients a favor and ask them.

If they give you ambiguous information, don't know or pretend not to know, chances are they are part of the problem. Open interoperability is the solution.

4. Higher Production

As I often state, a major reason I became a dentist is because when dentistry is done right, everyone wins. As we elevate care, we also raise our production and profitability.

If we provide higher quality treatment for more people, our team will feel more fulfilled and we will make more money.

This can be accomplished by relieving our teams of tedious, duplicative data collection, freeing them up to provide more treatment. Additionally, by having complete information and the ability to improve communication both within our teams and with outside collaborators, it will cost us less time, energy and money to deliver care.

Imagine how much easier it will be to make referrals and receive referrals, including referrals from our physician friends in the emergency room who are helping so many patients in need (as discussed in Chapter 1).

Speaking of helping those in need, if you haven't tried virtual consults for higher value cases yet, I would highly recommend it.

These patients who haven't been to the dentist in twenty years typically know they have large dental treatment needs, as they look at their missing teeth, caries and bleeding gums every day in the mirror. And someone that knows they have large dental needs often feels shame and anxiety and is looking for a way to understand their treatment options without being lectured.

The most convenient and least intimidating way to bring these patients in is to give them the ability to just snap a few pictures of their teeth and send them to you. Provide these patients with an easy, online process to connect with you 24 hours a day, 365 days a year, whenever they get up the courage to reach out. This process for virtual consults also allows you to respond when it is convenient for you.

This not only allows your large production cases to skyrocket in frequency, but it opens up new opportunities for a large demographic of patients to receive the care they desperately need.

5.   Higher Profitability

It is shocking how few dental practices actually know their profitability. I certainly did not fully understand my practices' profitability until I sold them.

If I could rewind the clock or travel back in time and give myself some advice on how to reduce my stress and improve my practice, I would figure out a way to track PROFIT, not just production, on a daily, weekly and monthly basis.

So much stress in my (and likely your) work life comes from producing more, only to wonder "where did all that money go?"

The best way to see what "dials" need to be tweaked in order to create more profits is to use an analytics platform that not only tracks revenue generated, but also tracks expenses that are easily categorized, providing immediate insights into your profitability.

I shudder to think of the countless hours I spent researching how to save $20 on some new composite or minor equipment purchase without realizing the thousands of dollars in production I was missing out on. Not to mention the people I could have been helping with that wasted time.

Also, remember that our biggest expense is our team's time, so in the vast majority of practices, automating and reducing a team's workload is the single most effective way to reduce expenses. Too many practice owners overlook this opportunity. Gaining insight into how your wages are related to your profitability makes this reality blatantly clear and easily actionable.

6. Dentistry Will Be More Fun and Fulfilling

Expanding automation through interoperability does not only make us more profitable and provide higher quality care—it also makes work more fun.

Do you, or someone on your team, really want to stuff a piece of paper into an envelope, stamp it and send it in the mail to see if someone will pay their bill? Make a phone call to remind someone of their appointment? Talk to some computer guy on the weekend to update your server or, heaven forbid, spend another tens of thousands of dollars on a new server and computers to run the latest update to a software platform that doesn't even work with other solutions?

Again, we have a good news/bad news scenario.

The bad news is that our reality is a painful one.

The good news is that you get to choose your pain.

On the one hand, you can choose either the relatively minor discomfort of doing the work to seek out solutions that solve the Dental Disorder in your practice and provide better quality care, more profits and a virtually future-proof practice that requires little to no IT company interference.

Or you can choose to propagate the painful present situation of upgrades, multiple logins and of unsecure data that is locked in a server prison, leaving you vulnerable to fines related to your inability to access information that is managed by you, the dental professional, and legally owned by your patients.

As I do, you may also distinctly remember the joy you felt when you got your first CAD/CAM system, CBCT machine, soft tissue laser or curing light. It's why we all love that "new phone feeling" and even that "new car smell." Getting new tech is just plain fun.

Through implementing interoperability in your practice, you can install, trial, implement and uninstall new apps with a single click, just like on your phone.

The fun way. The way it should be.

7. Inevitability

Interoperability is inevitable.

The 21st Century Cures Act has finally given it teeth, making possible a way of practicing that we all recognize should have been implemented long ago.

Switching software will be easy.

As a patient, you will be able to access your dental records

As a dentist, you will get all the information you need for new patients, as if they had been a patient in your practice for the last decade.

As an innovative software vendor, you will no longer need to pay extortionate rates and remain forever beholden to archaic juggernauts that don't understand the business they are in.

Interoperability is happening now. Just as you have the choice of either doing the light lifting to implement interoperability or suffering the pain of resisting the coming change, you have a choice of deciding when to jump on board.

You can be part of the solution today.

Or you can choose to prolong the pain that our teams, practices and patients currently feel.

Please choose wisely.

To find out how to implement important, inevitable interoperability go to dentaldisorder.com

13

THE CURE

"The path to success is to take massive, determined action."

- Tony Robbins

Problem: As the cure for Dental Disorder is to handle our patients' electronic health information in a way that is secure yet openly interoperable, we face significant challenges to making this all happen in a way that is both thorough and timely.

Solution: With a sense of urgency, leverage interoperability solutions that comply with existing Standards and regulations, and work to improve them consistently in a way that elevates our quality of care, enhances patient experiences and boosts dental practice profits, while also communicating the importance of interoperability throughout our profession.

The lack of data accessibility in dentistry is unique.

There has actually been a massive sea change within healthcare that has enabled physicians, hospitals and medical patients to have open and secure accessibility to the information that is required to provide higher quality care.

This change in medical electronic personal health data accessibility, however, has been far from perfect and has some large barriers to overcome, such as creating greater alignment on Standards, reducing regional differences and collaboration on or consolidation of competitive health information exchanges (or HIE's).

While we in dentistry are currently behind our medical colleagues when it comes to addressing the interoperability needs of our EDR's, we also don't have many of the barriers to implementation that exist in other aspects of healthcare.

Therefore, I believe strongly that dentistry could quickly become an example of ideal interoperability for the rest of healthcare, a model for others to mirror.

This is because we have more narrowly defined use cases for our data and the fact that we are just getting started in implementing interoperability means that we can learn from other initiatives that have paved the way for our industry.

Just as the iPod was not the first MP3 player, Airpods were not the first Bluetooth headphones and Tesla did not make the first electric cars, the technology that "gets it right" is often one generation behind the first attempts. This is where we are today with the Dental Disorder.

So, how do we address all the previous disorders that have been outlined up to this point? It comes down to three independent, but equally important initiatives: Standardization, innovation and education.

Standardization

- Intentful design that aligns an industry towards progress

Innovation

- Executing on the vision designed in a way that allows for easy implementation

Education

- Communicating the solution and its value to all stakeholders through clear messaging

3

Standardization

As outlined in Chapter 4, the first Standard to directly address dental interoperability is called ODIN: the Oral Dataset Interoperability Network. Through ODIN, we will align all of dentistry on not only how to structure dental patient data and securely store and transfer this vital information, but also on what information it makes sense to share with each provider.

Within the U.S., the critical data elements for a Standardized set of the broader health data classes and elements are defined within the United States Core Data for Interoperability (USCI). In dentistry, we must segment and share this data, along with dental-specific data, in a way that makes sense.

As previously discussed, a physician does not need to sift through all of a dental patient's data to provide the highest quality of care. A physician, for example, does not necessarily need to know if a dental patient has gingivitis.

ODIN defines the limited sub dataset of information to pass from dentistry to medicine and vice versa.

The information passed from an EDR to an EMR is defined within ODIN as the Dental Specific Summary or DSS, whereas information that is outlined to be shared from an EMR to the EDR is termed the DMHS, or Dental Medical History Summary.

ODIN addresses many of the shortcomings that exist in current medical Standards. For example, there are multiple medical Health Information Exchanges (HIEs) that, at the time of this writing, do not share complete information with each other. While this is being rapidly addressed, we have the opportunity to avoid this mess in dentistry by aligning on a single way to share information. A single Dental Health Information Exchange (DHIE) through the ODIN network.

Another concern that has become quite problematic in medical electronic health data exchanges is the verification of a patient's identity. Just as there are multiple HIE's in medicine, there are multiple patient identification systems.

We have addressed this through developing a system defined within ODIN called the ODIN ID, an Unique Patient Identifier (UPI) for dentistry. With this unified means to create and track a patient throughout their dental journey, we can be assured that the information we obtain about our patients is correct.

ODIN IDs can then be referenced and synchronized with other datasets that also belong to the dental patient, including medical records, financial records and so on.

Additional dental Standards work is needed, which is why we are working hard to uncover and address the areas of dentistry that require alignment within the

Dental Standards Institute (DSI) and ADA Standards workgroups.

Currently, we are working on developing Standards that address insurance adjudication, billing, payments and reporting, that redefine the elements of an EDR and that ensure Equitable Electronic Dental Record Access (EEDRA) for patients to have access to and agency over their dental records.

Every one of these Standards is not only made more possible, but also actionable and enforceable by existing regulation such as HIPAA and the 21st Century Cures Act.

While the 21st Century Cures Act is in just the initial phases of enforcement, a single incidence of any party blocking access to patient data can already incur a fine of up to $1 million. This reality promises to quickly popularize adherence to these Standards and regulations.

Therefore, while the topics discussed in this book may seem new to many today, I believe that they will soon be part of our daily lexicon and provide a new phase of more profitable, patient-oriented and more rewarding dentistry.

Innovation

Developing the structure for which we can create security, openness and accessibility to patient electronic dental information does no good if it is not implemented within at least one technology platform that elegantly and inexpensively allows this information exchange to occur.

Ideally, this interoperability platform would not only provide the "connective tissue" between all applications within dentistry and connect all other relevant applications (such as accounting and payroll applications), but it would also serve as an interconnected ecosystem by which dental practices, vendors and patients can easily select whatever software they desire.

As this did not exist in dentistry, I have partnered with one of the best developers and, at great expense of time, energy and money, worked to build this platform.

We call it Toothapps.

Innovation on this scale is not easy. Stated bluntly, the average dental technology company today could not make this happen. It is not because they are not talented; it is because they are software engineers, accountants, corporate leaders and managers. They are not dentists, hygienists, office managers and dental assistants. They understand software, not dentistry.

Dentistry is filled with examples of technology that just doesn't make sense. This is because most dental technology was created without clinicians in leadership positions.

The quintessential example of this is the fact that the largest practice analytics platform in dentistry was developed by an accountant, but it does not include expense data. Therefore, we have a situation where an accountant developed a platform that does not show practices' profits.

Any office manager who has lost sleep at night because their incredible production numbers from last month did not answer the question "where is the money to make payroll?" would not omit this key detail.

Any dentist that meets with their financial planner and has to guess the value of their largest investment, their dental practice, would include a practice valuation estimator as something that can be tracked daily.

Any company that claims to be innovative in dentistry should have a team of exceptional dental professionals leading their development and support. Otherwise, they are a group of people looking to profit from an industry they don't quite understand. Yet this remains the norm.

Dental innovation can only be at its best when led by dental professionals.

This just may be my opinion. However, I believe I have had as much experience and insight into this world as anyone in dentistry, so it is a highly educated opinion.

Education

You cannot implement innovation without education.

For a new idea to succeed, it needs to be designed well (Standards), crafted correctly (innovation) and then marketed and sold in a way that people can understand its value to them (education).

Education, therefore, is vital to the success of any endeavor. That is why I am so grateful that you have read this far!

As dentistry's demographics change and the pace of innovation exponentially escalates, getting access to efficient, well-organized online education will become more and more necessary for all dental professionals.

Over the course of the last two decades, I have given hundreds of lectures all across the country. In doing so, I have had the honor of meeting and becoming friends with many of the "greats" in our profession who do the same.

What struck me in early 2022 was the fact that all these phenomenal educators in dentistry could not wait to get back "onstage." I, on the other hand, fell in love with the ability to give a two-hour lecture to hundreds of people, then shut my laptop and go to my son's baseball game.

Online education is just so much more convenient and cost-effective. You can reach way more people in a way that is better for all involved.

As the increasing speed of innovation requires more education, reaching more people more frequently is a necessity. New technologies and procedures all require training to be effective, so we must strive to make continuing education more convenient.

Of course, this is not always possible. Some dental education needs to be in person, such as when rendering hands-on clinical treatment is part of the training. However, this will change. I have already been involved in developing some Artificial Reality and Virtual Reality (AR/VR) education that will very soon make it possible to be digitally present "in person."

I founded Upgrade Dental to be the best source of "what's new" in dentistry so that dental professionals could stay up-to-date with what they need to know in the world of dental innovation. At Upgrade Dental, we work with the most progressive faculty members and teams to deliver updates on Standards, innovations and practice leadership concepts that are easy to digest and implement.

Whether we can address Dental Disorder and break our patients' electronic dental information out of the data prisons they are currently locked in today is up to us all.

While DSI, Toothapps, Upgrade, the ADA and others can provide the structure, technology and education required to move dentistry forward to an improved future of higher quality care, enhanced profitability, more fulfilled teams and empowered patients, it is up to all of us to make the change.

The regulations are in place. The fines are being levied. Our patients' and our team's expectations are already there.

The promise of medical-dental integration is not possible without interoperability. Having one login for all your applications is not possible without interoperability.

Never having to pay for another integration or ridiculous IT fee, eliminating expensive "dental software taxes," being able to switch PMSs without being held hostage, automating supply ordering and having instant communication with everyone you work with are all possible today.

It just requires you to take the first, easy step.

AFTERWORD

Dentistry is at a crossroads.

We must move quickly to implement the innovations that are required in order to expand the security and privacy of and accessibility to our patients' vital electronic dental information. If we act now, dentistry can become a model of interoperability that the rest of healthcare can follow.

Our patient care will improve, our bank accounts will grow, our teams will be happier and healthier and our patients will feel the improvements in a fundamental way.

Maybe we can even go a week in our practices without hearing the dreaded phrase "I hate being here."

If we fail to act, however, we will expose ourselves and our profession to several risks. There will be fines, loss of patients' confidence, degradation of employee morale and increased propagation of the monopolistic, anti-competitive practices of large corporations that dominate our profession.

Instituting interoperability is easy and inexpensive. It will actually save money, time and hassle for everyone in dentistry. But it will not happen without you acting.

I get it. Dentistry is a difficult profession and running a dental practice requires wearing many hats. However, if you are like me, you wouldn't have it any other way. Dentistry is difficult because we dental professionals are in control of our own destinies. We collectively maintain autonomy over our industry and can guide it to a better place.

Throughout *Dental Disorder*, I have attempted to outline what I believe to be the biggest threats to this way of practice, as well as the solutions to these disorders.

Thank you for caring enough about dental patients, dental practices and the companies that serve them both to pick up and read this book. Very few will make it this far, so I am grateful to you.

Whether you are one of the heroes in the line of care for patients, a patient that advocates for others, an educator or a partner to the industry, it takes all of us to support our beloved profession and raise dentistry to a higher plane.

Together, we can address Dental Disorder and provide for secure, open interoperability. When we do, we all win.

ADDITIONAL RESOURCES

To join the cause of intently designing Standards that align healthcare to remove the bottlenecks to innovation and put patients first, go to:
DentalStandardsInstitute.com

To implement interoperability in your dental practice or dental group so that you can save money, comply with the 21st Century Cures Act and release yourself from the Dental Disorder, go to:
Toothapps.com

To learn what's new in dentistry, provide your team with online education that is devoid of fluff and learn how to become an Insanely Productive Dentist, go to:
UpgradeDental.com

To pursue the new way to grow the dental practice of your dreams and realize the power in adjusting your practice to the patient's perspective, go to:
ThePatientFirstManifesto.com

ACKNOWLEDGEMENTS

Thank you to the incredibly talented and inspiring team members at Toothapps and Upgrade Dental; Megan Hennen, Nate Johnson, Aleh Matus, Tim Koivisto and Abby Frey. You are the exceptional group that lead the BIG revolution in healthcare. I am honored to pursue excellence alongside each of you. This book and our progress in solving the Dental Disorder truly would not have been possible without you.

This book was also improved significantly through the detailed work of copy editor Haleigh Pouliot.

I owe a debt of gratitude to both the dental practice team members and patients that I have done my best to serve throughout my clinical career. I am especially grateful for the extraordinary dentists that lead Lake Minnetonka Dental: Drs. Cindy Perone, Ketan Patel, Julia Herman and Nicole Holmes.

Lastly, and most importantly, thanks to Tesa, Naiya and Miles for being the incredible people that you are and for your unwavering support.

ABOUT THE AUTHOR

Dr. Bryan Laskin is a Minnesota dentist and tech entrepreneur on a mission to help dental teams and patients break free of the "Dental Disorder" through innovation, education and Standardization.

A practicing dentist and owner of Lake Minnetonka Dental for over 20 years, creator of Upgrade Dental, Digital Nitrous and OperaDDS, Co-Founder of Toothapps, author of the Amazon best-selling book *The Patient First Manifesto* and host of *The Patient First Podcast*, Dr. Laskin excels at helping others integrate technology and teamwork into their practices. He serves as CEO and Chairman of the Board of Dental Standards Institute.

Dr. Laskin is an advisor to and investor in many of the most progressive healthcare companies. He is also a frequent keynote speaker.

To learn more about Bryan Laskin's key initiatives or to inquire about speaking engagements, go to bryanlaskin.com

Printed in the USA
CPSIA information can be obtained
at www.ICGtesting.com
JSHW022052310823
47340JS00009B/24